Baptists and the
American Civil War

CRUCIBLE
OF FAITH
AND FREEDOM

Bruce T. Gourley

© 2015

Published in the United States by Nurturing Faith Inc., Macon GA,
www.nurturingfaith.net.

Library of Congress Cataloging-in-Publication Data is available.

ISBN 978-1-938514-82-1

CONTENTS

*Publication of this book is made possible through gifts
from the following sponsors:*

Patrick and Carolyn Anderson, Beech Mountain, N.C.
Philip and Sharon Ball, St. Charles, Mo.
Don Brewer, Gainesville, Ga.
Caralie Nelson Brown, Raleigh, N.C.
David W. Bryant, Seneca, S.C.
Frieda Byrd, Macon, Ga.
Tony and Susan Cartledge, Apex, N.C.
Harvey Clayton, Raleigh, N.C.
Kenny and Shirley Crump, Ruston, La.
David Dawson, Lithonia, Ga.
Walter Draughon III, Waynesville, N.C.
Pat Ingle Gillis, Statesboro, Ga.
William Harris, Alexandria, Va.
Jim Jones, Macon, Ga.
Dan Mayfield, Chattanooga, Tenn.
Emmanuel and Emma McCall, Atlanta, Ga.
Bill and Carolyn McConnell, Knoxville, Tenn.
Roger and Suzii Paynter, Decatur, Ga.
Barry and Rebecca Pierce, Taylorsville, N.C.
Charles and Elizabeth Qualls, Atlanta, Ga.
Virgil and Judy Quisenberry, Central, S.C.
Louise and Roy Runyan Jr., Jonesboro, Ark.
Ken and Kathy Russell, Calhoun, Ga.
Ken Sehested, Asheville, N.C.
Clem and Carole White, St. Petersburg, Fla.
Tim Willis, Clemson, S.C.

FOREWORD

My childhood assumption was that everyone grew up climbing on cannons and stone monuments — and that picnics and hikes were best suited for the wide expanses of a military park dotted with historical markers.

Saturdays might call for climbing up the west side of Lookout Mountain. After a lunch break at the historic Cravens House, where the famed "Battle Above the Clouds" had played out, we would push onward to the top for an impressive view from Point Park.

Lazy Sunday afternoons were often spent tossing Frisbees or footballs with friends in an open field near the 85-foot, stone Wilder Tower with its circular staircase. Our pursuit was more of fun than history — although we were surrounded by it constantly.

That narrow childhood perspective and those youthful experiences came from being born within a cannon shot of the Chickamauga Battlefield Visitor Center — and growing up all around the varied parcels that make Chickamauga & Chattanooga National Military Park the largest of its kind.

Just east of the park, my home community — including the church and elementary school I attended — bears the name of Henry Van Ness Boynton, who drove the effort to establish the first national military park there.

A Union officer, Boynton had received the Medal of Honor for his actions in the nearby Battle of Missionary Ridge. However, I don't recall ever being told that our nice little Southern community was named for a Yankee.

Proximity to the battlefield was extremely close, yet the harsh realities of the Civil War seemed far removed. The pristine park grounds belied the carnage that had occurred there less than a century before my birth.

While the monuments, markers and museum exhibits told in great detail the horrors of the costliest two-day battle of the entire war, such statistics felt distant from my daily, personal experiences.

At times, however, I did wonder what life was like for my ancestors and others there who lived through such a trying time. But my thoughts were more on the physical struggles they faced than anything philosophical, political or theological in nature.

Questions about what Baptist Christians were thinking, saying and doing at such a time were never raised. There were no serious inquiries into why American Christians plundered each other, with each side claiming a divine mandate.

The 150th anniversary of the war provided a grand opportunity to consider precisely what Baptists — North and South — were saying from their pulpits, in the press and through official resolutions from that time. And Dr. Bruce T. Gourley was the perfect person to bring such perspectives to life.

Making good use of careful and significant research, he has creatively taken a chronological approach using primary sources. There is much in this volume to be learned — and to long remember.

What do these persons have in common? Robert Smalls, Thomas Hill Watts, Basil Manly Sr., Gov. Joseph Brown, Gov. Sam Houston, Isaac Taylor Tichenor, Crawford H. Toy, and Frank and Jesse James.

The answer: They are just a few of the many Baptists who had a role in the American Civil War. Most went on to great prominence in politics, religion or education. The latter two became known for behavior not learned in Sunday school.

So read — or read again — these firsthand accounts of how Baptists on both sides sought and claimed divine favor and righteousness. The lessons are as plentiful as the statues and markers that dot the many battlefields where the devastation has given way to peaceful fields and quiet woodlands.

—John D. Pierce
Executive Editor, *Baptists Today* news journal
Publisher, Nurturing Faith Books

A WAR LONG COMING

The road to the American Civil War began with the introduction of slavery into the American colonies in the mid-17th century. Slavery was confined to Africans, as English common law prohibited the enslavement of white persons.

Human bondage entered the colonial experience in Virginia, a colony whose economy depended upon agriculture. For the cultivation of tobacco and other crops, slave labor was much cheaper than indentured servitude — which included both blacks and whites — or wage labor. The practice grew quickly, encompassing Southern and Northern colonies and putting an end to indentured servitude.

By 1720, slaves represented 30 percent of Virginia's population and 70 percent of South Carolina's population. New York led the way in slavery in the North, with 15 percent of the state's population enslaved. Whereas slaves worked the fields of the South, in the North they worked on farms, as tradesmen and in homes, while on a larger scale the North benefited from the buying and selling of slaves.

On the eve of the American Revolution up to 5,000 slaves were imported into the colonies on an annual basis. Out of a total of roughly half-a-million slaves in the colonies, some 90 percent lived in the Southern states. Free blacks existed, but largely in the North and in few numbers.

Following victory over the British, the original 13 colonies set about the task of establishing a national union on a permanent basis. Slavery, however, proved to be a stumbling block. The Northern colonies were already turning against slavery, with Vermont leading the way by abolishing the practice in 1777, and others soon following. Influential, large-scale slaveowners, on the other hand, controlled the politics of the Deep South and were not about to give up the source of their great wealth: slave labor.

Northern delegates to the Constitutional Convention soon realized that the creation of a strong central government would necessitate compromise with Southern slaveowners. Northern slave-owning delegates along with some from Virginia and Maryland insisted that slavery was inconsistent with liberty, freedom and morals, and thus should be abolished in the Constitution. In response, John Rutledge of South Carolina spoke for most Southern slaveowners when he declared, "Religion and humanity have nothing to do with this question [of slavery]."

Viewing themselves as an aristocratic class, wealthy slaveowners insisted that freedom and liberty belonged to whites only. Delegates from the Deep South states of South Carolina and Georgia stood ready to walk away from the proposed union if their demands for the permanent establishment of black slavery were not met, thus holding the Constitutional Convention hostage and forcing the North to acquiesce to their demands.

As a result and despite the promise of equality embedded within the nation's Declaration of Independence, human bondage was written into the Constitution in the form of each black slave being counted as three-fifths of a person for legislative representation and taxing purposes. This arrangement provided the South with greater proportional representation in the nation's capitol, resulting in the Southern dominance of the U.S. government until the Civil War. In addition, the South secured the extension of the Atlantic slave trade for 20 additional years, thus ensuring enough time for the slave population to continue growing of its own accord. Apart from the Constitution, Southern delegates forced the enactment of a runaway slave clause mandating the return of escaped slaves to their owners.

Southern slaveholders scored an additional major victory in 1791 in the enactment of the Second Amendment to the United States Constitution, which reads: "A well regulated Militia, being necessary to the security of a free State, the right of the people to keep and bear Arms, shall not be infringed." The amendment was added at the insistence of slaveholders who wanted assurances that they could raise militias to put down slave rebellions.

A number of slave revolts occurred in the late 18th and early 19th centuries, including an especially ambitious, attempted insurrection in Charleston, S.C., the epicenter of pro-slavery ideology. In May 1822 Charlestonians caught wind of what became known as the Vesey revolt, named after Denmark Vesey, a free black and a prominent Christian leader among Charleston's black population.

Vesey recruited more than 100 co-conspirators who planned to lead a violent uprising against slaveowners in the Charleston area, free as many slaves as possible, and then commandeer local ships and sail for the free state of Haiti. Word of the insurrection leaked, however. Vesey and his co-conspirators were arrested, and many put to death. Afterward, Charleston officials voted to raise a local militia to protect the city and surrounding area from future slave rebellions. The result of that decision led to the creation of the South Carolina State Arsenal, otherwise known as the Citadel, which in 1842 became the South Carolina Military Academy.

Beyond the creation of the pro-slavery U.S. Constitution and the Second Amendment, one final development sealed the opposing views of freedom and liberty between the North and South: the 1794 patenting of Eli Whitney's cotton gin. The device allowed for a much faster processing of cotton, a profitable Southern agricultural commodity extensively dependent upon slave labor. In 1800 the South produced some 200,000 bales of cotton annually, a number that rose to more than 4,000,000 by 1860. Some 4,000,000 slaves worked mostly in the cotton fields of the South by 1860, planting, tending and harvesting America's largest export product.

Although slavery was abolished from the Northern states by 1804, the North nonetheless bought much of the South's cotton, processing the raw product in textile mills and generating considerable wealth. The public's conscience increasingly struggled to reconcile the dichotomy. Christian leaders black and white during the height of a period of religious revival known as the Second Great Awakening spearheaded a growing abolitionist movement that reached a critical mass about 1830. The ascent of abolitionism in the North paralleled the firm establishment of cotton as the dominant cash crop of the South, which in turn further galvanized Southern politicians in the nation's capital to resist, with all means possible, any attempt to curtail, much less abolish, the institution of black slavery upon which the Southern economy heavily depended. South Carolina in 1832 voted to withdraw from the Union in protest over a national tariff act that wealthy slaveowners believed would reduce their cotton profits, backing down only when the tariff was watered down.

As the Southern position on slavery hardened and Northerners increasingly gravitated toward abolitionism, many Baptists of the South initially expressed affinity with Northern views. A minority and persecuted sect in the mid-18th century, Baptists of the South in particular were largely a rural, lesser-educated and lower socioeconomic group. Few white Baptists had the means to own slaves. Baptist preachers in the decades prior to the Revolution often admonished slaveowners to free their slaves. Many slaves voluntarily joined white Baptist churches, in part appreciative of the Baptist view of the spiritual equality of blacks and whites. Neither heavily vested in nor benefiting significantly from the institution of slavery, into the Constitutional years most white Baptists of the South seemingly remained largely ambivalent or opposed to slavery. In some instances blacks, slave and free alike, formed their own congregations under the watchful eye of the law. In 1789 the Virginia Baptist General Committee declared that "slavery is the violent deprivation of the rights of nature, and inconsistent with republican government," a "horrible evil" that should be abolished by "the use of every legal measure."

The First Amendment's establishment of religious liberty for all and church-state separation, however, provided opportunity for the minority Baptists of the South to move toward both the religious and socioeconomic mainstreams characterized by strong pro-slavery currents. In 1793 Virginia Baptist leaders reversed their earlier anti-slavery course and declared that slavery was neither a moral nor religious issue, but rather a political matter. An 1805 Virginia state law requiring that slaves obtain written permission of their masters in order to join a congregation put an end to slaves in that state freely joining Baptist congregations, creating ever greater distance between whites and blacks.

As Southern laws in many states further cemented the bondage of blacks during the first and second decades of the century, white Baptists throughout the South grew rapidly, adding to their ranks a growing number of wealthy slave-owners. Many churches benefited from the surging profits of plantation owners whose fields of rice and cotton were worked by slaves, resulting in the enlargement of many church buildings, edifices often both financed and constructed by slave labor. Into these churches slaveowners sent their slaves to worship, balconies having been constructed for their segregated seating. In areas with large slave populations, Baptist congregations and their pastors rose to places of community and civic prominence, with South Carolina leading the way.

By the 1820s many white Baptists of the South had tacitly accepted the racial caste system of the Southern states. The next step was for white Baptists to move from quiet approval of black slavery to formal, theological ownership of the practice. That moment arrived on Dec. 24, 1822, in Charleston, S.C.

On that day and in the wake of the failed Vesey rebellion, Richard Furman, arguably the most prominent Baptist minister in the entirety of the South, wrote a pointed letter to the governor of South Carolina. In his capacity as president of the Baptist State Convention of South Carolina, Furman assured the governor that white Baptists of the South embraced the "right view" of black slavery. White Baptists believed that God had blessed South Carolina in the thwarting of the Vesey insurrection, Furman declared. The minister offered his assurances, on behalf of his fellow Baptists, that the enslavement of the black race was a biblical, moral and Christian practice ordained of God for the well-being of an inferior race. The state of South Carolina, in short, could depend upon white Baptists to wholeheartedly support the benevolent institution of black slavery.

Furman's letter signaled a unity of elite white Baptists and government leaders in the South, moving Baptists from a position of passive acceptance of black slavery to a position of theological, and hence religious, affirmation. In the decades following, Baptists and Presbyterians and Methodists of the South bathed slavery in a literal reading of the Bible, preaching slavery from the pulpit and in denominational literature. In so doing, they intentionally positioned themselves against Northern counterparts who advocated for abolitionism on the basis of a contextual reading of the New Testament that dismissed biblical acceptance of slavery as an ancient, discredited practice and instead focused on Jesus' command to love one's neighbor as oneself (Matt. 22:36-40) and on Paul's declaration that all persons are equal in the eyes of God (Gal. 3:28).

Religion represented a significant dimension of Northern opposition to slavery, but so did class economics. Apart from religious sentiments, Northern Baptists and other Christians were alarmed that Southern slave labor distorted and harmed the wage labor market both South and North, magnifying white poverty in both urban and rural areas.

This biblical-infused and economic-laden battle over freedom for all versus freedom for whites only grew increasingly hostile until in the 1840s the Methodists, Baptists and Presbyterians of the South began breaking apart from their Northern counterparts in defense of black slavery. Baptists split in May 1845 when prominent Baptist slaveholders gathered in Augusta, Ga., and voted to form the Southern Baptist Convention in order to ensure the continued enslavement of blacks, thus preserving the economic benefits accrued to their churches and mission efforts from slave labor.

While the regional division over slavery had by now existed for decades, the splintering of denominations signaled that differences over slavery had risen to crisis proportions. Political events in the 1850s subsequently escalated tensions as Southern states demanded the right to expand slavery westward and Northern states resisted such efforts. In addition, Northern states claimed states rights in refusing to enforce fugitive slave laws. Southern states dismissed Northern rights and instead claimed their own states rights in demanding that Northerners return their escaped property. Against the backdrop of political polarization came increasing violence between pro- and anti-slavery advocates in Washington, D.C., in the Border States, and on the Western frontier. The increasingly complicated political nuances of the heated slavery debate roiled the two-party national political system. Politicians on the fence regarding slavery were forced to choose sides. The Democratic Party largely opted for a pro-slavery position while the Whig Party waffled, creating an opportunity for an anti-slave party to emerge: the Republican Party. By 1860 the Whig Party was effectively reduced to political rubble and an anti-slavery, Baptist-raised, backwoods lawyer from Illinois by the name of Abraham Lincoln emerged as the presidential candidate of the Republican Party.

As the worlds of religion and politics collided spectacularly over the issue of slavery, the ever-skyrocketing economy of the South pulled an astonishing amount of wealth southward, wealth that accumulated in the hands of a relatively few large slaveowners. Massive wealth inequality among white Southerners led to the decline of the white male population in the 1850s South as poor whites moved North and West in search of jobs. By 1860 the South was home to the 10 richest counties in America and most of the nation's millionaires, the wealth clustered along the South Carolina coast and Louisiana's Mississippi River delta — regions of fertile soil and massive plantations worked by hundreds of thousands of slaves.

Abraham Lincoln's presidential victory in the fall of 1860 convinced South Carolina's elites that further negotiations with Washington, D.C., were fruitless. Republicans led by their illegitimate "black president" would insist upon the containment of slavery to the South and, eventually, to the abolishment of the practice altogether. In order to protect their riches now and in the future, wealthy slaveowners had to propel the South to leave the Union.

On Dec. 17, 1860, in the sanctuary of the First Baptist Church of Columbia, S.C., the state's wealthy slaveowners assembled for the purpose of leading South Carolina to secede from the United States. Three days later, the secession convention having been moved to the slavery capital of Charleston due to an alleged smallpox outbreak in Columbia, delegates issued a Declaration of the Immediate Causes Which Induce and Justify the Secession of South Carolina from the Federal Union. The document pointed to disagreements over slavery as the foundational reason for secession, villifying the North for its abolitionist sentiments and refusal to help slaveowners recover runaway slaves, and for daring to brand slavery as sinful. White freedom, the delegates insisted, depended upon the enslavement of blacks. Not all Southern whites agreed that secession was necessary, but the white elites of South Carolina were not about to give up their freedom to own slaves. And they were determined to bend the will of the larger white South to their view.

Secession had begun. Other Southern states would follow in the months ahead. Prominent Baptist pulpits and newspapers of the South, in addition to those of other denominations, blessed the disunion, speaking forcefully for white liberty and black enslavement. A new nation was to be birthed, a godly nation in which black slavery, willed of God, would last in perpetuity. And if need be, the South would take up arms to preserve their slavocracy.

A line was thus drawn over the future of a long-discordant nation. With the Union and human freedom at stake, an untried president of a fledgling political party for whom only 40 percent of voting Americans had cast a ballot prepared to take a suddenly weakened office. But by the side of the country lawyer-turned-president stood the Declaration of Independence, the United States Constitution, the North's industrial might, a superior number of white males, and a mature abolitionist movement with deep and broad support in the religious community.

No less important, from across the great regional divide the daily prayers of millions of enslaved black individuals — the Baptist faith predominant among those holding church membership — fervently petitioned God for freedom, prayers that helped empower resistance to the oppressors in ways subtle but real. Upon the faith and bravery of the oppressed hinged the outcome of the coming war.

NOTES

This volume, originally published as a series of articles in *Baptists Today* from 2011-2015, is a condensed version of the five-year, daily digital journal project, *Baptists and the American Civil War: In Their Own Words*, written by Bruce T. Gourley and located online at civilwarbaptists.com. The website features approximately 1,800 articles arranged by date and exploring the lives, thoughts and actions of Baptists during the Civil War — white, black, Native American; North and South; Southern, Northern (American), Primitive and more.

Also included on the website are primary source and secondary source material information from which the articles in this print book rely. To locate specific sources for a given month in this book, refer to the online daily articles for that month at civilwarbaptists.com.

1861

The election of Abraham Lincoln to the presidency of the United States in November 1860 prompted slaveholders in South Carolina to call a state secession convention in December 1860. Other Southern states soon followed, collectively forming the Confederate States of America in order to preserve African slavery. Photo from the Library of Congress.

Following South Carolina's secession from the United States, six more states secede this month: Mississippi, Florida, Alabama, Georgia and Louisiana.

In Southern statehouses and elsewhere, Abraham Lincoln is belittled as the "black president," his party as "Black Republicans." Secession convention delegates decry the abolitionist North and vow to defend "African slavery." Among the delegates are many Southern Baptists, ministers and politicians with secessionist and pro-slavery convictions. In some cases, Baptists are among the ranks of state officials. Georgia is led out of the Union by Gov. Joseph Brown, a Southern Baptist layman.

The outcomes of the secessionist conventions, however, mask complexities. In Georgia, the popular vote is against disunion, an outcome suppressed at the time (and not uncovered until the 1970s). Carrying on as if authorized by voters, delegates to the state's secessionist convention gather and decide for secession.

One of several states this month in which the popular votes for secession are close, Georgia's reticence reflects widespread feelings of caution harbored by many white Southerners. While most seemingly support black slavery and oppose the Northern abolitionist movement, large numbers of poor whites, impoverished due to the wealth inequalities of the South's slave-based economy, see secession for what it is: an attempt by powerful slaveholders to preserve their own riches. White elites from the comforts of their plantations worked by vast numbers of slaves have long assured their poor brethren that solidarity lies in skin color, insisting that the slave economy is good for all whites. Many common folk, however, remain unconvinced. Significant if minority anti-slavery sentiment is present in the mountainous regions of the South where the soil is poor, life is hard and there are no plantations.

As in most Southern states, many prominent Baptist ministers in Georgia echo pro-slavery politicians, assuring an uncertain public that secession is the only way to preserve the God-ordained institution of African slavery. Samuel Boykin, Baptist minister and editor of the Macon-based Georgia Baptist *Christian Index*, reminds his readers why secession is necessary: "It is plainly perceptible that slavery is authorized by the Bible and by the God of the Bible, and it is only as thus authorized, nay enjoined, could we defend and perpetuate it." Speaking rhetorically of the differences South and North over slavery, Boykin asks, "Can light & darkness dwell together? Can irreconcilable enmity and cooperation dwell together?"

On the last Sunday of the month, Ebenezer W. Warren, pastor of the First Baptist Church of Macon, Ga., Boykin's home church, preaches an unashamedly pro-slavery sermon to a packed audience. Titled "The Scriptural Vindication of Slavery," Warren's sermon assures white and black church members alike that black slavery is "a vital element of the Divine Revelation to man" and a "blessing to humanity." The enslavement of the black race is "ordained and perpetuated by God" for all time, and the enslaved are "peaceful and happy." The Old Testament, Christ and Apostle Paul all affirmed black slavery, and nations must submit to God's will in the matter. Abolitionism is "religious fanaticism" and must be resisted at all costs.

Among the few prominent Baptists of the South who consistently oppose secession, ultimately refusing to become reluctant disunionists as do some others, is Alfred Dockery, a U.S. congressman from North Carolina and a slaveholder. Amidst growing public calls for secession within his state, Dockery laments, "The disunion mania which now pervades the breasts of so many Southern men progresses with unprecedented rapidity, and like the devastating tornado threatens to prostrate all in the dust."

Another prominent Baptist who opposes secession is Texas governor Sam Houston. As his state's secession convention assembles near the end of the month, Houston refuses to back down in his beliefs, his convictions on a certain collision course with the pro-secession sentiments of most convention delegates.

Dockery and Houston aside, most white Baptist elites support secession in order to preserve black slavery. Nonetheless, such sentiments represent only a portion of the Baptist family in the South. Of the South's four million slaves, more are of the Baptist faith than of any other formal religious persuasion. Their voices legally muted and their bodies often scarred and violated by the hatred and lusts of their owners, black Baptists are united in their desire for freedom from bondage. For generations they have endured enslavement, their masters and white ministers insisting that bondage is their God-ordained lot in life. But they know otherwise. God desires freedom for all people. God is on their side. One day, God will redeem his people from bondage, as he once before did in the Old Testament exodus. Perhaps Abraham Lincoln will be the new Moses God uese to free his people.

From afar, President-elect Lincoln reads with alarm of the swelling secessionist fever throughout the South. What will happen next he does not know. He does, however, represent the majority voice of Northern voters, voters who elected him on a platform of freedom and liberty for all. Raised in an anti-slavery Baptist church, convicted that God wills freedom for all humanity, and as a lawyer committed to upholding the Union that is the United States of America, Lincoln is determined to do what is necessary to both maintain national unity and fulfill America's promise of liberty for all.

On the first day of the month Texas becomes the seventh state to secede from the Union. Gov. Sam Houston, a Baptist, remains opposed to disunion.

While formal hostilities are yet two months away, Confederate forces are already marshalling and probing Union defenses of Southern coastal forts. An early Confederate triumph is the capture of Fort Pulaski near Savannah, Ga.

Dozens of Baptists have played significant roles in events thus far. In the South, many Southern and Primitive Baptists serve in secession conventions. Northward, rhetoric from abolitionist Baptists is increasing.

In publications and public speeches, Southern politicians and preachers proclaim the defense of black slavery as the primary rationale for seceding from the Union. Among white Baptists in the South clamoring for secession and proclaiming God's will for black enslavement is Ebenezer W. Warren, pastor of the First Baptist Church in Macon, Ga., who on Jan. 27 preached — to a full house — a sermon titled "The Scriptural Vindication of Slavery."

This month the *Macon Telegraph* and *Christian Index* publish the sermon for their readers, here excerpted:

> Slavery forms a vital element of the Divine Revelation to man. Its institution, regulation, and perpetuity, constitute a part of many of the books of the Bible …. The public mind needs enlightening from the sacred teachings of inspiration on this subject. … We of the South have been passive, hoping the storm would subside. … Our passiveness has been our sin. We have not come to the vindication of God and of truth, as duty demanded … it is necessary for ministers of the gospel … to teach slavery from the pulpit, as it was taught by the holy men of old, who spake as moved by the holy Spirit. … Both Christianity and Slavery are from heaven; both are blessings to humanity; both are to be perpetuated to the end of time. … Because Slavery is right; and because the condition of the slaves affords them all those privileges which would prove substantial blessings to them; and, too, because their Maker has decreed their bondage, and has given them, as a race, capacities and aspirations suited alone to this condition of life. …

Among Alabama's state secession delegates is James DeVotie. One of the most respected preachers in the state, DeVotie, currently pastor of the First Baptist

Church of Columbus, Ga., was previously pastor of Montgomery First Baptist Church, Tuscaloosa First Baptist Church, and Siloam Baptist Church in Marion.

In addition, DeVotie had been a voting delegate at the founding meeting of the Southern Baptist Convention in Augusta, Ga., in 1845; helped establish Howard College (now Samford University); and held a variety of elected positions in state and national Southern Baptist life. A lifelong advocate of public education in Alabama, he also served as editor of the *Alabama Baptist*.

DeVotie soon serves as a chaplain in the Confederate Army, refusing to accept payment for his services, on the principle of separation of church and state.

In Montgomery, Ala., on Feb. 4, representatives from the seven secessionist states join forces to create the Confederate States of America. Jefferson Davis — Mississippi U.S. Senator and former Secretary of War — is elected as temporary president. A Provisional Constitution is enacted on Feb. 8.

Following the creation of the Confederacy, Samuel Boykin in the Feb. 27 edition of the *Christian Index* voices a grand and glowing vision of the prospects of the Confederacy and black slavery:

> We will absorb Central America and the contiguous states of Mexico, not by … bloody … war … but by the generous attractions of our superior civilization and purer religion. … When these golden visions become realities … then will the proudest nations of the earth come to woo and worship at the shrine of our imperial Confederacy.

Renowned Georgia Baptist minister Adiel Sherwood offers, in the Feb. 20 edition of the *Christian Index*, his own observation: "The slaves enjoy soul liberty, a much higher privilege than mere bodily freedom."

Yet not all white Baptists in the South celebrate secession and black slavery. Union sentiment is strong in the mountains of Georgia and North Carolina and throughout Tennessee. Tennessee Governor Isham Harris on Feb. 9 calls for a state vote on whether or not to send delegates to a state convention that would decide on secession. Itinerant Tennessee Baptist minister Jesse Cox records in his diary: "I walked one mile and voted against the state voting a convention to secede from the Union." The vote fails, although Tennessee later becomes the last state to secede and join the Confederacy on June 8.

March arrives with Jefferson Davis, former U.S. Senator from Mississippi, presiding over the Confederate States of America. Currently comprised of Deep South states only, the Confederacy hopes to attract some of the peripheral, or Border, states.

Virginia, home to much Union sentiment, is undecided regarding secession. Tennessee's ultimate position is far from certain. Arkansas and North Carolina have not yet rallied for disunion.

In Texas, the last state to secede at this point, the governor — Sam Houston, a Baptist — is dismissed this month from the governorship for refusing to take the oath of allegiance to the Confederate States of America.

The Confederate States are united in declaring that slavery is the reason for the formation of their Confederacy. The CSA Constitution expressly invokes the favor of "Almighty God," while Georgia — under the leadership of a Southern Baptist governor, Joseph E. Brown — declares itself a "Christian nation."

Basil Manly Sr., a large slaveholder, a leading voice in the formation of the Southern Baptist Convention and a founder of The Southern Baptist Theological Seminary, has established himself as the chaplain of the Confederacy. Having delivered the prayer at the inauguration of Jefferson Davis, Manly now relies on his Calvinist theology to assure fellow Southern Baptists that God's hand guides the new Southern nation.

Indeed, many Baptist pulpits and newspapers in the South pointedly appropriate God and the Bible in the fight to preserve African slavery.

Sitting quietly in church balconies, slaves say nothing that their masters might overhear, but at night in their crude cabins express their anxieties to one another. Few can read, but many clutch to the belief that the biblical God of deliverance is on their side and dream of a day of redemption.

As Abraham Lincoln's inauguration as the 16th U.S. president takes place on March 4, many white Southerners express open contempt toward the president and the United States. Lincoln's agenda, they are certain, is the abolishment of slavery.

Lincoln comes from a Baptist background, having grown up in a Northern Primitive Baptist family.

Mary Beckley Bristow, a member of Sardis Primitive Baptist Church in Union, Ky., sums up the feelings of many white Baptists of the South as she comments on Lincoln's inauguration in her diary:

[Lincoln] has it in his power (for us poor mortals to look at the matter) to do much of good or evil, and if we judge him by the silly, foolish speeches he made on his route [to his inauguration] and the pitiful, cowardly manner in which he approached the Capitol, slipping there in disguise, we have but little reason to hope for good. I would defy a "Philadelphia lawyer" to guess at what his intended policy will be from his inaugural address, whether he will give us peace by acknowledging the independence of those States that have seceded, now known as the "Southern Confederacy," or not, as he ought to do, we can give no idea. For my own part I believe he does not intend it. I believe him to be one of those deceitful, hardheaded persons who would overturn a world (if they could do it without personal detriment) to accomplish their fanatical bigotry. I imagine Lincoln to be such a man as the witch burners of Salem, Massachusetts, without Cotton Mather's sense to go on it, but none the less dangerous because of being feebleminded. May the Lord, if consistent with his will, save our country from a civil war.

We shall be fighting a double battle, against slavery at the South and against prejudice...at the North....

Frederick Douglass, *Douglass' Monthly*

Photo by John Pierce.

APRIL 1861

In early April, Confederate army volunteers throughout the Deep South prepare for what is widely viewed as an imminent war between North and South. Samuel Boykin, editor of Georgia's *Christian Index*, on April 3 calls upon white Southern Baptists to support the Confederacy:

> Whether the secession of the plantation states was justified or not — whether the Government of the Union has violated the Constitution and oppressed the South and imperiled our institution of slavery, and therefore made Southern life insecure, or not ... we see ... a special interposition of Providence. Behold what God has wrought!

Fort Sumter, off the coast of Charleston, S.C., proves to be the trigger that starts the war when Confederate forces bombard the fort on April 12 and force the Union to surrender the structure two days later.

U.S. President Abraham Lincoln, relieved that the South fired first, presses the Border States to remain in the Union, calls for army volunteers, and pronounces a blockade of the South. In turn, Lincoln's call to arms prompts Virginia to secede on April 17, becoming the eighth state to do so. Arkansas, North Carolina and Tennessee remain uncommitted.

As the month draws to a close, Georgia Baptists meet in Athens for their annual convention and issue a statement "on the present political crisis" that declares:

> Whereas, the state of Georgia, in the legitimate exercise of her sovereignty, has withdrawn from the Confederacy known as the United States of America; and, for the better maintenance of her rights, honor and independence, has united with other States in a new Confederacy, under the name of the Confederate States of America; and whereas, Abraham Lincoln, the President of the United States, is attempting by force of arms, to subjugate these States in violation of the fundamental principles of American liberty; therefore,

> Resolved, By the members of the Baptist Convention of the State of Georgia, that we consider it to be at once a pleasure and a duty to avow that, both in feeling and in principle, we approve, endorse and support the Government of the Confederate States of America.

Resolved, That while this Convention disclaims all authority, whether eccle-siastical or civil, yet as citizens, we deem it but a duty to urge the union of all people of the South in defence of a common cause; and to express the confident belief that, in whatever conflict the madness of Mr. Lincoln and his government may force upon us, the Baptists of Georgia will not be behind any class of our fellow citizens in maintaining the independence of the South by any sacrifice of treasure or of blood.

Resolved, That we acknowledge with devout thankfulness to Almighty God, the signal favor with which, up to this time, He has blessed our arms and our policy …

Resolved, That the Confederate Government be requested to invite the churches of all denominations within the Confederacy, to unite in observing days of fasting and prayer.

Northern Baptists conversely claim the righteousness of the Union cause. In 1884 an early historian of the Narragansett Baptist Association of Rhode Island (that state being the original home of Baptists in colonial America), founded less than a year prior to the Civil War, recalled how the organization's 20 member churches responded to Fort Sumter and the resulting war over black slavery:

Before a year had passed, Civil War burst forth in the land as suddenly and as unexpectedly to most as the tornado on a delightsome summer afternoon. The thunders of Sumpter fell upon the ear like that from lightning in a clear sky; its fall was as the descent of an angel from on high calling with clarion tone, to arms! The churches heard the summons; they recognized the mandate of the Supreme, and promptly obeyed. Their younger sons, clad in the full panoply of war, and remembering what Inspiration saith, "the powers that be are ordained of God" and "therefore he that resisteth the power withstandeth the ordinance of God," what their fathers had suffered to secure the price-less heritage they enjoyed not only through the turmoils of war, but from imprisonment and bonds and stripes, and what their Master had endured that whosoever believeth may have eternal life, at once entered the held, enthusi-astically singing, "As He died to make men holy let us die to make men free."

And thus, Baptists South and North, in addition to many taking up arms, from the beginning of the war square off in a verbal contest to define and defend freedom and liberty

Hostilities now official, the month of May is occupied with preparations for coming battles. North and South, war is the talk of the citizenry rural and city.

The uncommitted Border States remain critical to the fortunes of both the United States and the Confederate States. Nowhere are citizens more divided than in Kentucky.

Pulpits and churchyards are not unaffected by the war talk. On the first Sunday of the month, members of Kentucky's Old Cane Spring Baptist Church (located in Madison County, south of Lexington) gather for a day of worship and fellowship. A participant records the day's events:

Old Cane Springs appeared to be a God-fearing and God-loving community. There was preaching at the Cane Spring Church as usual. Rev. William Rupard, a young Baptist preacher from Clark County, had been engaged as minister. The first Sunday in May was expected to be a big day, and the usual preparations were made to entertain those attending who might live at a distance. Lambs, pigs, and chickens had been slaughtered by the dozens, and when the congregation began to assemble, it was evident that no unnecessary preparation had been made.

In a very short time the church was filled with ladies, except the "amen corner" and the extreme rear of the church. The yard was about as full as the church. Men gathered in various parts of the yard, and as one passed among them he heard nothing but war and preparation for war being discussed. ... The opposing views of the North and South were freely advocated and it was evident that the peace-loving and law-abiding citizens of Old Cane Springs and vicinity were ready to take up arms in defense of one or the other of the sections.

When the services were over, those who had heard the sermon came out either lauding or condemning the preacher, who had spoken of the people of the South as Rebels, bent on dissolving the Union of the States. His utterances on this point were soon known by the crowd on the outside, some of whom received them with condemnation while others approved; and excitement ran high. One man said in a loud voice, "No more of his preaching for me. No true preacher knows anything in his pulpit but Christ and Him crucified."

Most all of the members who owned slaves were grievously offended at the preacher's remarks. Major C.F. Burnam, an attorney from Richmond, who was present, congratulated the preacher on his defense of the Union. His statement, however, was overheard and caused him to be condemned as much as the preacher.

… Men of the community were fast taking sides and excitement ran high. Those with much property and many slaves sympathized with the South, while most of those with small homes and no slaves were for the North.

Meanwhile, in St. Louis, Mo., the Second Baptist Church is divided. In late April, the church's pastor, Dr. Galusha Anderson, had preached the first pro-Union sermon in the Border State city.

Church members in the weeks following take sides on the issue, as some Southern sympathizers in the city resort to violence. A church window is broken and a deacon shot.

One city newspaper editor writes scornfully of Galusha's sermon under the headline, "The Devil Preaches at Sixth and Locust."

Galusha remains resolute. Some families leave the church never to return, although in the coming years the church emerges stronger than ever.

Southward, the Southern Baptist Convention convenes in Savannah, Ga. The "lawless reign of terror at the North," delegates proclaim, is waging "a warfare of savage barbarity, to devastate our houses and hearths with hosts of ruffians and felons."

Southern Baptists pledge to fight back. Summoning "every principle of religion, of patriotism, and of humanity," messengers pledge their "fortunes and lives in the good work of repelling an invasion designed to destroy whatever is dear in our heroic traditions; whatever is sweet in our domestic hopes and enjoyments; whatever is essential to our institutions and our very manhood."

Therefore, "we commend to the churches represented in this body, that they constantly invoke a holy and merciful God to cover their [soldiers] head in the day of battle, and to give victory to their arms."

At the same time, Southern Baptists remain committed to evangelizing their slaves: "There is no class of people among us that more sincerely appreciate the efforts of our missionaries than the slaves that work our soil. Let us, then, give them the pure Word of Life that has elevated them so far above the condition of their race in the mother land."

JUNE 1861

Two months after war is declared between South and North, and in the absence of any meaningful battlefield engagements thus far, the Confederate and American public harbors a somewhat romanticized version of a war based on feelings of regional righteousness and pride.

Julia A. Sanford, a young Baptist woman in Forsyth, Ga., captures the positive mood characteristic in much of the South. In her "beautiful diary" that her fiancé sent her from his army post in Virginia, she writes:

> Wednesday, June 26 — What a good and refreshing Shower ... We may look for health and harvest. How good and great is our God!!! Everyone is looking forward to a speedy peace. So may it be.

Closer to the front lines, however, Mary Beckley Bristow, a member of Sardis Baptist Church in Union, Ky., laments news of a few minor preliminary skirmishes in nearby Virginia:

> O, what an awful situation our once happy country is in. War, dreadful, devastating war, with all its horrors is all around us. Old Virginia, the Mother of Kentucky, has had several battles fought on her soil. The invaders seem disposed to subjugate and destroy all who dare oppose their bigotry and fanaticism.

Bristow's words are a bit premature, as the first major battle of the war does not take place until late July. Yet few anticipate the full scope of the enormous carnage that lies ahead.

Soldiers, having volunteered to serve their countries, prepare for a war most believe will end quickly. The young army volunteers bring with them hopes and dreams. Some will survive the war, their futures defined by the great conflict.

Harrison Woodsmall, future Baptist minister and educator, leaves Indiana State University to join the Union's 14th Indiana Regiment. During the war he serves with distinction, attaining the rank of major in the 115th Indiana Regiment.

After the war, Woodsmall enrolls in The Southern Baptist Theological Seminary and works among freedmen in the South, first as an employee of the Georgia Baptist Convention, and later on behalf of American (Northern) Baptists.

In 1878, Woodsmall becomes the first president of the Alabama Baptist Normal and Theological School at Selma for African Americans.

In the pre-war South, whites and blacks typically worshipped in the same congregation, albeit in segregated seating. Sometimes, blacks were allowed to have their own congregation, under close supervision of a white mother church. Yet the war quickly frays the racial dynamics of church life.

The white First Baptist Church of Nashville, Tenn., in January 1861, had established a "Colored Baptist Mission" in Edgefield (East Nashville). Served by a free black preacher, George Dardis, the black Baptist congregation ministered to area slaves and freemen under the ever-watchful eye of a white committee. Yet upon Tennessee's secession from the Union on June 8, the First Baptist Church immediately discontinues the Colored Mission.

As the white South's ironclad grip on black slavery slowly loosens in the coming years of war, white Baptists' attempted control over black spirituality will follow suit.

Fort Pulaski, Georgia. Photo by Bruce Gourley.

Near Washington, D.C., on July 21 beneath a dawning Sunday morning, the war begins in earnest. Under pressure from the Northern public to march on the Confederate capital of Richmond, Va., President Lincoln orders Brig. Gen. Irvin McDowell southward, where his Union army encounters Confederate troops led by Brig. Gen. P.G.T. Beauregard.

The two armies square off in fields and woods near the town of Manassas, initiating the first major conflict of the Civil War. Baptists serve on both sides.

News of the battle spreads as the armies clash throughout the morning hours. In northern Kentucky, Mary Beckley Bristow hears cannon fire announcing the battle:

> This is a lovely morning, but my heart is sad and restless; have heard the cannons roaring at Cincinnati. I know full well that if they are not deceived by their dispatches, as they have been several times, the roaring of federal cannon brings no good news from the side on which my sympathies are enlisted, the side of liberty and right as I firmly believe.

On the battlefield this day the Union army, initially gaining the upper hand, is forced to retreat late in the afternoon, suffering defeat. Victory is cheered throughout the South; Northerners are dismayed and bewildered.

Yet starker than defeat and victory is the human cost of the battle: Among the 5,000 casualties, 460 Union and 387 Confederate soldiers lie dead.

Five days later, on Friday, July 26, the South Carolina Baptist Convention convenes in Spartanburg. The first resolution passed by delegates thanks God for the victory at Manassas:

> Resolved, That we heartily concur in the recommendation of our Confederate Congress, to unite in making our late signal victories the occasion of special thanksgiving to God, by appropriate religious services on the approaching Sabbath...

Another resolution voices confidence in God's favoritism of the Confederacy:

Resolved, That, in the present peculiar condition of our political affairs, it becomes us thus to assure our beloved country of our sympathies, prayers and thanksgiving on her behalf; that so far as we can understand the remarkable openings and guidance of Divine Providence, we have but received, in almost every instance, the merciful blessing of our God, as approbation upon the plans our State and Southern Confederacy have deemed it best to adopt; ... we can but rejoice in the oneness of our brethren of this State in prayer and effort to defend our homes, our liberties and our Churches, and encourage them to be assured that, as hitherto, putting our faith in God, though each of us may have much to bear, yet the rod will not finally rest upon us, but that in this most unrighteous and most wicked attack upon our otherwise peaceful homes, the wickedness of the wicked will return on their own heads.

The following Sunday, one week after Manassas, is a time of rejoicing in many Southern Baptist congregations. As black slaves quietly watch from their segregated perches in church balconies, preachers affirm the righteousness of the Confederacy and the liberties of white citizens for whom sons, fathers and brothers are fighting.

Soberness, however, marks many Baptist worship services in the North. The cause of liberty for all men has been dealt a setback. Yet firm are the convictions of many on the home front, buttressed with a certainty that God and righteousness are on the side of the Union.

In community emotions are openly expressed, but in quiet moments lurking anxieties grip the minds of many. As night falls over the broken land this Sunday evening, soldiers on both sides think of their families and wonder what lies ahead.

On the home front, as lamps and candles are snuffed out in thousands of Baptist homes North and South, the grieving of lonely wives, sisters, young children and aged parents alike mingles with the pressing darkness.

Yet among enslaved Baptists despair and despondency have long been a way of life unchosen, a darkness greater than night. While the Baptist faith in its Southern expression offers a faint echo of the fervency and emotion of slaves' ancestral religions and provides an otherworldly hope that transcends earthly shackles, Southern white divines insist that the Bible's God created blacks for bondage.

Rarely taught to read or write and often cut off from formal communication with outsiders, few Baptist slaves are aware of the full extent to which many of their spiritual kin in the North are committed to liberating them from the darkness of their physical bondage.

AUGUST 1861

The South, having chosen to go to war with the North in order to preserve a slaveholders' society, now faces the dual tasks of defeating the Union and suppressing Southern dissent.

As many as 25 percent of Southern white families own at least one slave, while 1 percent or less of slaveholders own most of the South's slaves. The 1 percent, in turn, owns the vast majority of Southern wealth and controls the region's political processes. Directing the affairs of the South, their money and power trump potential opposition from common whites and ensure the ongoing enslavement of African Americans.

Even as large-scale slaveholders during the war use their power to further increase their wealth, the regional culture of white supremacy serves as a balm over the financial chasm between slaveholders and poor whites — for now.

Nonetheless, many rural white Southerners living in regions largely devoid of plantations even now choose to support the Union over the Confederacy. Such is the case of East Tennessee, which by a 2-1 margin in June voted against secession.

Sunday, Aug. 11, is hot and hazy in Tennessee's Stockton Valley. Some 150 attend worship at the Union Baptist Church. After morning services, the women gather in small groups on the church grounds.

Inside the church building, 34 Baptist men — common folk farmers and craftsmen — regroup to discuss a solemn question: Should they remain at home and quietly resist the Confederacy, or join other East Tennessee dissenters in fleeing to Kentucky to join Union ranks? Even as they talk, Confederate forces are approaching, intent on suppressing rebellion in the valley.

Nine days later following a treacherous journey, the men are in Kentucky. Along with hundreds of other Tennesseans, they enroll in the newly formed 2nd East Tennessee Infantry (Volunteer), U.S.A.

Like the white Baptists from Tennessee's Union Baptist Church, an increasing number of African slaves are seizing opportunities to flee to Union lines. In response, this month the United States passes the Confiscation Act of 1861, allowing federals to seize property used in the Southern insurrection.

In effect, slaves (legal property) forced to participate in the Confederate war effort are granted freedom behind Union lines.

Meanwhile, in Kentucky, the Campbell County Association of Baptists issues a circular letter for distribution among member congregations. The subject of the war is heavy on the hearts of the delegates as they lament the disunion of the nation. Kentucky's status as a Border State with mixed loyalties is evident in the anguished feelings of delegates:

> Might it be said that the nineteenth century has prostituted the purity of the gospel to so base a purpose as arming brother against brother? Or if this must, in truth, be acknowledged, shall it be that the elements of the Campbell County Association must carry out the same intolerant spirit? God forbid! If Christian love and fellowship were as the spirit of the gospel would have them, this could never be: yet the fellowship of churches (not in this Association) has been entirely destroyed by the introduction of political issues ... how fearful the ground upon which any brother stands, if he feels in his heart a rising hatred towards a brother whose greatest fault may be honestly differing upon the politics of the day.

No major battles are fought this month, as generals of both armies plot strategy and train soldiers. Among notable events, North Carolina's Cape Hatteras falls to Union forces, Maryland remains with the Union, western Virginia moves to form a separate state, and martial law is declared in Missouri, resulting in the freeing of slaves in the state.

For some Baptists, life goes on without major disruptions. Revival season begins in the South. Women primarily attend, alongside men who are not fighting in the army. The war adds urgency to revivalists' invitations. As is customarily the case, church rolls increase during revival season.

Northward, Augustus Hopkins Strong is ordained pastor of First Baptist Church of Haverhill, Mass., his first pastorate. After the war, Strong becomes president of Rochester Theological Seminary and a leading Baptist theologian of the 19th and early 20th centuries.

In the broader picture, the antebellum era hardened regional Baptist theology, cementing biblical literalism in the South while in the North accelerating the embrace of critical biblical scholarship expressed in contextualized scriptural interpretation.

In addition, the early months of war heighten the trend of women's numerical dominance in church attendance. Yet in August 1861, the transformative force of the Civil War has just begun.

SEPTEMBER 1861

September is the month of Baptist associational meetings, two- to three-day events normally filled with sermons, mission reports, Sunday school reports and other church-related business. Other than in churchyard talk and private conversations, rarely do events and topics outside the realm of church business surface in associational meetings.

This month, however, church yard talk and formal meetings of Southern Baptist associations gravitate toward the one topic on everyone's mind: the new Southern nation and the war being fought to preserve it.

Gatherings of two associations in Georgia are typical of many throughout much of the South.

Meeting at Traveler's Rest Baptist Church in Macon County, messengers of the Rehoboth Baptist Association insist, "We honestly believe that in this great struggle for all that is dear to us as a people, we have the approving smiles of Him who rules at his will the destinies of nations … and His sure protection to our friends and relatives upon the tented field."

The Flint River Association, meeting at the Shiloh Baptist Church in Monroe County, "heartily" endorses the "separation from the North and South and the formation of the Southern Confederacy." Pledging themselves to the "defence and support" of the Confederacy, they credit the summer's military successes to God and "sincerely and earnestly pray that He will guide us in all our efforts and sustain us in all our righteous purposes to a successful and triumphant determination of this war."

Most Primitive Baptist associational gatherings, however, avoid discussion of the war. The contrast between Southern and Primitive Baptists in the South speaks to a wartime divide between the two groups. While many Southern Baptists push separation of church and state to the background in fervent support of Southern Christian nationalism, Primitive Baptists by and large stand firm upon their faith heritage of church-state separation.

Many associational meetings in the Border States also address the war. Meeting at Dry Creek Baptist Church in Kenton, Ky., the North Bend Baptist Association bemoans current events:

> Never before in the history of our country have external circumstances furnished elements of distraction better calculated to disturb the peace, spirituality and fellowship of the churches, than those which now environ us.

We are in the midst of a political revolution the most astounding, a civil war the most desolating and appalling, and a wide spread excitement which threatens devastation and ruin to all we hold dear in life. As intelligent freemen, heirs to the common heritage of civil and religious liberty, we cannot look upon the ominous events now rapidly transpiring around us without agitation and the most painful solicitude.

While anarchy and confusion in many parts of the country have repressed the dictates of reason and justice, giving rise to the wildest disorders, the bitterest denunciations, and the most rancorous feeling of enmity between neighbors, friends and countrymen … Let us cultivate fervent love for one another, and with a sleepless vigilance give ourselves to prayer that "the God and Father of our Lord Jesus Christ" may keep us "in perfect peace;" that He may *overrule* the present storm, and cause "all things to work together for good to them that love Him, and who are the called according to his purpose."

Nearly four more years of this "present storm" of hatred, death and destruction lie ahead in the war over African slavery and the struggle for God's divine favor.

Baptists from both the United States and the Confederate States claimed the Bible and God were on their side. Photo by Bruce Gourley.

The battles unfolding in these autumn days are minor compared to the earlier Battle of Bull Run / Manassas. Nonetheless, this month in Loudoun County, Va., the second largest battle in the Eastern theatre to date — the Battle of Ball's Bluff — takes place.

Still glorying over their earlier triumphs, the Confederates again emerge victorious. Making matters all the worse for the seemingly hapless United States of America is the death of Oregon Senator Edward Baker during the battle. The only sitting American senator ever killed on the battlefield, Baker had raised a brigade on the West Coast and returned East to fight the enemy.

As annual associational Baptist meetings in the South convene this month, Christian nationalism rides the swell of a rising Confederacy. Baptists of the Chattahoochee Baptist Association in North Georgia make clear their convictions in a report on "State and Country":

> Whereas, Abraham Lincoln is endeavoring to subjugate the Southern states contrary to the Constitution which he has taken an oath to carry out to the letter and, if he is successful, he will deprive us of our rights, religious and politically bequeathed to us by our forefathers, and will confiscate our property and do violence to our persons to such an extent that death itself would be preferable;

> Resolved, that, while we look to the God of Justice, we will defend our rights with our blood and our treasure at all hazards, and to the last extremity, and we believe that every friend of the Southern Confederacy will do likewise.

Further westward, the Mississippi Baptist Association adopts a resolution regarding the war:

> Resolved, That Saturday before the first Lord's day in November be recommended to the churches composing this Association as a day to be devoted to fasting and prayer in view of the state of our Confederacy and the war that is being waged against us.

As white Southern triumphalism and prayers for the Confederacy carry the day, cooler heads are fewer and less vocal. Among the outliers is Leonard Stephens, longtime Kentucky Baptist layman and state politician, who in a private letter to his brother lends a measured voice to the nationalist rhetoric:

> You & I my Brother have had nothing to do with the bringing on of this war, But we are certain to have a good deal to do with its consequences, for if it lasts much longer our Great Grand children will be taxed all their lives to pay its expenses. Does it not behoove every man then that has influence to endeavor to induce the Southern States to return to their allegiance as loyal citizens.
>
> Please give me your views candidly in regard to this whole matter, & if we differ or if you do not agree with me, we will still be Brothers & have the same affectionate feelings for each other as we have always done. ...

Both sides claim the moral high ground. The South has come too far to entertain the possibility of backing down. Yet in the battle for freedom for all versus freedom for whites only, the North's superior financial resources and manpower, once fully deployed, will prove formidable.

The First Battle of Bull Run / Manassas, a victory for the Confederates, set the tone for the first year of the war. Photo by Bruce Gourley.

NOVEMBER 1861

Eight months into the war, the South is clearly winning the conflict that has now claimed thousands of lives. While the North grows restless, the Confederates continue racking up battlefield victories.

White Southern Baptists, rejoicing in the success of the Confederate war effort, remind their fellow white Southerners to abstain from sin (African slavery not counted as such) in order to ensure God's continued blessings upon the Southern nation. Convening for their annual meeting, Alabama Baptists issue the following statement:

> ... We feel obliged as lovers of God and of our country, to acknowledge the stress in which we now find ourselves, but above all, we do recognize the hand of God in leading us into our present condition. ...

> We wish also, to express our gratitude to God for having given us a chief magistrate who has, in all his official acts and proclamations, recognized the dependence we all feel on the Almighty Ruler of the Universe for success in the present struggle, for every blessing we enjoy.

> And we trust our whole people will strictly observe the days appointed by civil authority for fasting and prayer, and that they will humbly approach the throne of grace, to confess their sins before God, and to supplicate blessings upon our country and our rulers, our people and our armies, and all those interests which are dearer to us than life itself; and that the Prince of Peace may gain new victories. ...

One of the Confederate-proclaimed days of fasting and prayer takes place this month. In Georgia on the appointed day, Mercer University professor (and future Mercer president) Henry Holcombe addresses the Georgia legislature:

> The scoffer and the infidel may question the sincerity of the christian, or if not, they will perhaps be surprised to learn that to his mind the most cheering evidence of our success in this war is this acknowledgment of God so wide spread in the hearts of the people. ... This then is the chief reliance of the christian patriot in this emergency. It is gratifying to see that this devout and

proper spirit so generally prevails, and it should be the great aim of all who love God to cultivate and cherish it. ...

Here then is joyful news to thousands of Christian patriots who burn with desire to aid their country's cause, but who know not what to do. All you have to do is to be good, and in being good you are doing good; and in doing good you are securing the favor of God and contributing your share towards enlisting Him on the side of our armies. ... My countrymen, we are certain of success in this war if we but use the right means. ... Let us "seek first the kingdom of God and his righteousness," and trust that all other things will be added ... the days of Millenial glory would come, and the whole world would be subject to the gentle reign of the Prince of Peace!

Against the backdrop of growing Christian nationalist euphoria among Southern Baptists, a scholar-in-the-making is adapting to a new lifestyle as an infantryman in Virginia's Norfolk Light Artillery Blues.

Crawford H. Toy, an accomplished young man and one of the first students of The Southern Baptist Theological Seminary, is an ardent supporter of the Confederacy. In addition to his duties as a soldier, Toy in time also becomes a chaplain in Gen. Robert E. Lee's army.

His friends in the army write of his devotion to the study of languages, and Toy is known to pull out his books during lulls in battles. Toy survives the war, and the world remembers him as an outstanding Harvard professor.

Yet Toy's journey from the battlefield to Harvard is first a Baptist story. In 1869, SBTS hires the 33-year-old Toy as an Old Testament professor. Popular with faculty and students, he remains at SBTS until 1879, at which time his increasingly "liberal" views concerning the historical accuracy of the Old Testament lead to his firing, paving the way for his Harvard career.

Toy thus becomes representative of the next major salvo in the Southern Baptist war over biblical literalism. An approach to biblical interpretation that sanctioned African slavery and led to the war to defend the practice, biblical literalism in the post-war years trains its guns upon modern science as represented by Charles Darwin and the theory of evolution.

This war continues to the present day in Southern Baptist life, as 21st-century Southern Baptist theologians and historians yet dismiss Toy as a heretic.

DECEMBER 1861

December arrives. The armies, unable to maneuver or fight because of weather-related communication and supply chain problems, settle down to wait out the long, cold months of winter.

Tens of thousands of men spend Christmas far from home, away from families and loved ones. Some live in canvas tents, struggling to stay warm. In many instances, idle troops build log cabins as winter quarters. In the winter camps the days are filled with drills, gambling, drinking alcohol, eating and occasional preaching.

Not surprisingly, Baptists on the home fronts South and North talk of the war and worry about the health and morality of loved ones serving as soldiers.

Among white Southerners, hatred of the "abolitionist" North is now at a fever pitch. J.R. Graves, famed Landmark editor of the *Tennessee Baptist*, remains under a cloud of suspicion. A Northern transplant, Graves has long been accused of being an abolitionist, and by now has spent years trying to refute his critics. This month Graves prints a letter in the *Tennessee Baptist* written by a Texas Baptist identified as B.F. Burroughs:

> There is no religious interest anywhere, hardly; this unholy war has absorbed everything else. I see at every corner, and in every lane and alley, the Secular and Methodist papers are publishing and boasting of their preachers and lay members' bravery; and what valiant soldiers they all are, to read their accounts! One would think that the Confederate army was composed of the Methodist denomination alone, gathered to fight this Abolition war, of which they had a great deal to do in the bringing of it on, by publishing to the world in their law-book, (the Discipline), as strong Abolition sentiments, ever since the days of John Wesley as ever were proclaimed from a Northern Abolition pulpit. What would have been your fate if you and your brethren had published such sentiments? They would have taken you to the rack, or the stake, and burned you because you had the moral courage merely to express your thoughts. Dr. Howell & Co., I reckon, will drop the charge of Abolitionism against you now, since your faith and works on that point are known, and read of all men. What will they resort to next, since their marriage to Method-ism, and all other sorts of Isms, to make sure of your destruction and the downfall of the Tennessee Baptist; but surely they are kicking against the pricks, or at least they are certainly beginning to think so. They have gained just such victories

as the Lincoln army has in every engagement of any note that they have had with the Confederate army.

Most white Southern Baptists remain certain that African slavery is God's ordained will for the black race, and are convinced that the Confederate army is God's army. A Baptist minister in Richmond thus enthuses: "Never was an army, since the days of Cromwell in which there was a more pervading sense of the power of God."

Northward, some Baptist preachers ratchet up patriotic themes as the year draws to a close. In some cases, church congregations offer the use of their buildings and lands to the Union army. Such is the case of the First Baptist Church of York, Pa.

George M. Slaysman, pastor of First Baptist York, and his congregation earlier in the year allowed the Duquesne Grays Pennsylvania unit to use church buildings as barracks for battlefield training. Upon completion of their training, the soldiers seek to pay the church for their use of the facilities, but Slaysman refuses payment. In appreciation, the Grays soldiers gift the church with a Communion table Bible.

For his part, Slaysman remains ardent in his support of Union soldiers, and plays a prominent role in the building of a U.S. Army hospital in York. Later, in the summer of 1862, the Baptist pastor volunteers his services as the chaplain of the newly-created 130th Pennsylvania Regiment.

Baptist ministers serving as army chaplains North and South in almost all instances (other than active soldiers who also assume chaplain responsibilities) refuse government pay, instead depending upon their own resources or funding from Baptist congregations and/or denominational bodies. Particularly in the South, the refusal to accept government pay for army chaplain services is one of a few ways that Confederate Baptists, caught up in the fervor of Christian nationalism, remain faithful to their heritage of church-state separation.

1862

Soldier deaths in 1862 mounted both North and South, including in the Battle of Fredericksburg. Photo by Bruce Gourley.

JANUARY 1862

Military movements are restricted during the winter months, although not altogether forsaken. On Jan. 1, Confederate Gen. Thomas "Stonewall" Jackson, taking advantage of spring-like warm weather in Virginia, sets out with 9,000 troops on a maneuver to push federal forces from the Union-supporting Western portion of the state.

Designed as a campaign of preparation for spring battle plans, the effort is partially successful. Federal forces that the Confederates encounter mostly retreat in surprise, abandoning their winter camps with supplies and food intact. Although the weather turns frigid during the expedition and thwarts larger-scale ambitions, by the end of the month Jackson is successful in seizing control of the Shenandoah Valley and Allegheny ranges.

Despite continued Union setbacks, volunteers are now pouring into U.S. army ranks and preparing for battles certain to commence upon the coming of spring.

Winter does not deter the newly-formed 8th Michigan Infantry, as this month they assemble for a sacred consecration. A veteran of the War of 1812, Abel Bingham gazes down over the young men before him. The pastor of the First Baptist Church of Grand Rapids, Bingham as a military veteran knows war and peace. The old soldier also knows spiritual struggle.

Following the War of 1812, the New Hampshire native for 27 years served as a missionary to the Indian tribes in the Upper Peninsula of Michigan, his work marked by hardship and marginal success. In his most enduring legacy as a missionary, Bingham established what later became known as the First Baptist Church Sault Ste. Marie. Yet this occasion is especially poignant. His gaze lingers upon one soldier in particular: his son-in-law. Doubtlessly, Bingham is thinking of the soldiers and their families as he offers a prayer:

> May the Lord of Hosts be your Leader, ever inspiring both officers and men with true patriotism, and a confidence reliance on the Divine arm in every emergency, and make you brilliantly triumphant in every combat.

Victory in "every" engagement is a bit much to ask of God, yet the 8th Michigan serves valiantly throughout the war as the regiment traverses both the Eastern and Western theaters of engagement.

The high cost of war, however, is becoming all too real for many home-front Baptists North and South. Representative of many stories is a belated death notice that appears in this month's *Tennessee Baptist*:

Died in the hospital at Richmond, Virginia, L.B. Oldham, son of John and Clarissa Oldham, now living in Lavaca City, Texas. The subject of this notice was born May 5, 1839, in Carroll County, Mississippi. Moved with his parents to Western Texas in the fall of 1854, and in August 1860, returned to Mississippi, and joined the Confederate army in June last — took the measles which terminated his life Oct. 5, 1861. He leaves behind him a father, mother, sisters, and three brothers, and many friends to mourn his loss; but we weep not as those who have no hope, for three days before his death he professed, and we have no doubt obtained, the religion of our Lord Jesus Christ.

The above testimony was received from his nurses that attended on him while sick.

Apart from death, troubles are arising in Confederate army camps, as related by a Baptist soldier from North Carolina who writes to that state's *Biblical Recorder*:

I had heard of the immorality in a campaign life before as being very great, but not the half has been told. Profanity, both among the officers and privates, seems to be the ruling passion. ... Intemperance and gambling come in for their fair share. ... How we hope to prosper with the severest denunciations of the Bible upon these popular vices, seems to be presuming upon God's goodness! ... We have no Chaplain to our Regiment. I have not heard a sermon in camp for several months — men sicken and die without any spiritual counsel. Vice in every form, the most hideous, stalks abroad without warning.

J.H.F.'s observations are shared by numerous other Southern Baptist soldiers during the war. Confederate Baptists, so often espousing Christian nationalism, thus confront a disconnect that few choose to openly recognize: How can the army of God's chosen nation be characterized by overwhelming evil? This uncomfortable, often unspoken question lingers throughout the war.

FEBRUARY 1862

As snow blankets the ground in the Upper South, ebullience over last year's Southern battlefield victories slowly fades. Prospects of an alliance with England and France, a union of nations that would almost certainly guarantee Confederate victory over the United States, are dimming.

Failed diplomacy, however, is merely one of many troubles. Soldier deaths from illness are mounting. Nashville is occupied by Union forces. Confederate exports are severely hampered by a Union blockade, crippling the region's economy and raising the prospect of financial collapse. In the face of pervasive uneasiness, white Southerners hope that the resumption of battles in the spring will renew Confederate momentum.

Seeking to rally the South, Southern Baptists ratchet up their nationalistic rhetoric. *Christian Index* editor Samuel Boykin declares:

> Warriors of Jesus! can ye sleep in times so perilous to the cause of your master, and dangerous for your own souls and so prostrating to vital Christianity?

> Awake! awake! shake off your slothfulness, and let our southern Zion, like Samson of old, burst asunder the chords with which our subtle adversary has bound us, and, by our attention to duty, by our holy zeal, by our earnestness in religion, by our stern opposition to all wickedness in ourselves and others, and by our interest in all that pertains to the Kingdom of our Blessed Savior, seek to reform the nation, promote vital godliness in all classes, extend the borders of Zion, and draw down upon our churches and Confederacy the blessings of Almighty God. ...

> [Southern Baptists'] Opportunities for benefiting themselves, their race and the cause of God, must not be allowed to flit by and be lost forever.

Within Zion, however, Boykin's hint of internal wickedness is perhaps understated. An anonymous correspondent writing to the *Biblical Recorder* peels back the curtain on camp life in the Confederate Army:

> [the camps are] wholly given up to wickedness ... the number of apostacies, when this war closes, will astonish and mortify good men everywhere. ... Those who go into camp without firmly established moral principles, in fact,

without a heart full of vital godliness, rarely escape being plunged into the vices that surround them. ...

... the subject is made still more gloomy because christian people seem not to know how to check this flood of iniquity...

In the midst of nationalist fervor on the one hand and concern for sin in the camps on the other, Baptist editors, denominational leaders, pastors and laity of the South alike debate the future of the Confederacy. Most are convinced that their nation, despite any shortcomings and in spite of setbacks past and yet to come, is ultimately invincible because it is blessed of God.

Yet voices of caution persist, casting shadows over prophetic certainty. One Baptist writer, acknowledging Northern successes in blockading the Confederate coast and threatening communication lines within the South, reflects on what might happen:

We believe that truth and right and justice and God are on our side, but fighting in such a sacred cause as this, we can not hope for success, unless we use the legitimate ends for its attainment. We can not expect God to crown us with victory, if we are careless and indolent, and forgetful of Him. It is only when we acknowledge and realize our dependence on him, and make faithful use of the means of defence which he has placed in our hands, that we can over come our foes. If we do this for the future, we may expect success; otherwise we may look for the mortification and humiliation of defeat.

Such words of concern are not without merit. Many Baptist congregations in the South are closing their doors. The *Tennessee Baptist* newspaper ceases publication this month, its demise brought about by the Union occupation of Nashville. At the same time, the Southern Baptist Convention, acknowledging a steep decline in funding, scales back mission efforts and focuses attention on work among Confederate soldiers. The rapid retrenching of Baptist life in the South, in short, portends a long and troubled struggle for the soul of God's chosen nation.

Despite all these troubles, Feb. 22 is a day of celebration in the South as Jefferson Davis is promoted from his position as provisional president of the Confederacy to that of president. During the inauguration ceremony he kisses a Bible given to him by *Tennessee Baptist* editor J.R. Graves.

Spring arrives, and with it Union hopes for a reversal of fortune. U.S. President Abraham Lincoln, sensing the impatience of the Northern public, relieves Gen. George McClellan of supreme command of the Union Army. McClellan's new responsibility is the Army of the Potomac, with orders to attack Richmond, the Confederate capital. Thus begin preparations for the Peninsular Campaign.

Meanwhile, the Confederate and United States elevate naval warfare as the first clash of ironclad ships occurs. Off the coast of Virginia, the *C.S. Virginia* sinks two wooden Union warships and then fights to a draw with the *U.S.S. Monitor*.

White Baptists of the South continue their defense of the Confederacy — on the battlefield, on the home front, in the Baptist press, in the world of politics and sometimes in church services.

Bibles are on the minds of Southern Baptists, or more precisely, the lack of scriptures among Confederate soldiers. This month in Augusta, Ga., Christian leaders from across denominational lines gather for the Bible Convention of the Confederate States of America. Determined to move beyond current fragmented and ineffective Bible publishing and distribution efforts in the South, delegates create the Confederate Bible Society. W.D. Rice, General Superintendent of the Baptist Colportage Board, is chosen to represent the Bible Society among Southern Baptists.

In addition to Bibles, Baptists contribute bells to the Confederate cause. One such instance is noted by the *Richmond Dispatch*:

> The congregation of the Second Baptist Church in this city have set an example that may challenge emulation, but for self-sacrificing patriotism cannot be excelled. They met not long since and by unanimous vote gave their church bell to be cast into cannon to be used in the public defence. To show that this was not an empty promise made for effect, they immediately had it taken down to be put to the use indicated. At the same meeting at which the resolution above stated was passed, it was determined to subscribe a sum sufficient to purchase enough metal to add to that in the bell to form into a battery to be called the Second Baptist Church battery.

Not to be outdone, Northern Baptists contribute to the Union cause in ways similar — and unique. Perhaps the most notable moment this month among Baptists of the North occurs on a Wednesday night at the First Baptist Church of

Philadelphia. A guest speaker, 28-year-old Joseph Gilmore, a graduate of Brown University and Newton Theological Seminary, preaches on Psalm 23, focusing on the sentence, "He leadeth me beside the still waters." As Gilmore later recounted:

> Those words took hold of me as they had never done before, and I saw them in a significance and wondrous beauty of which I had never dreamed.
>
> It was the darkest hour of the Civil War. I did not refer to that fact — that is, I don't think I did — but it may subconsciously have led me to realize that God's leader ship is the one significant fact in human experience, that it makes no difference how we are led, or whither we are led, so long as we are sure God is leading us.
>
> At the close of the meeting a few of us in the parlor of my host, good Deacon Watt son, kept on talking about the thought which I had emphasized; and then and there, on a blank page of the brief from which I had intended to speak, I penciled the hymn, talking and writing at the same time, then handed it to my wife and thought no more about it. She sent it to the *Watchman and Reflector*, a paper published in Boston, where it was first printed. I did not know until 1865 that my hymn had been set to music by William B. Bradbury. I went to Rochester [New York] to preach as a candidate before the Second Baptist Church. Going in to their chapel on arrival in the city, I picked up a hymnal to see what they were singing, and opened it at my own hymn, "He Leadeth Me":

He leadeth me! O blessed thought!
O words with heavenly comfort fraught!
Whate'er I do, where'er I be,
Still 'tis God's hand that leadeth me!

Sometimes 'mid scenes of deepest gloom,
Sometimes where Eden's bowers bloom,
By waters still, o'er troubled sea,
Still 'tis His hand that leadeth me!

[Refrain]
He leadeth me, He leadeth me,
By His own hand he leadeth me:
His faithful foll'wer I would be,
For by His hand He leadeth me.

The gloom of these times is all too real, and Baptists North and South hope and pray that God is leading their respective nations.

As the month of April dawns, the Confederacy reels from Union advances in the state of Tennessee. Andrew Johnson now serves as the military governor of Tennessee, appointed by U.S. President Abraham Lincoln.

U.S. Gen. Ulysses S. Grant advances into the southwestern portion of the state. Disillusioned but not entirely defeated, the Confederates regroup in western Tennessee. Stopping Grant's advance is imperative.

On April 6, two Confederate armies launch a surprise attack on Grant's army, which is leisurely encamped near Shiloh Baptist Church, a small log church inland from Pittsburg Landing on the Tennessee River. Confederate forces, some 55,000 strong under generals Albert S. Johnston and P.G.T. Beauregard, push Grant's army back toward Pittsburg Landing. Thousands of Union soldiers are captured in the bloodiest day of the Civil War to date.

As night falls, the Confederates are certain they have bested Grant. Yet Union reinforcements arrive in the evening, and the next morning Grant launches a counterattack, driving the Confederates back to the Shiloh Baptist Church, where they make a last stand before retreating in defeat.

The Union thus wins a great victory, while the Confederacy suffers a shocking defeat. Grateful for victory, President Lincoln decrees a national day of Thanksgiving. Recoiling from defeat, the Confederate Congress passes the South's first Conscription Act.

Beyond the momentary emotions, the carnage of the Battle of Shiloh is staggering: 10,000 Confederate casualties and 13,000 Union casualties. One year into the war, any hope of the conflict ending with one great battle is lost. North and South now realize the immensity of the challenges ahead.

In the wake of Shiloh, Rev. S. Dryden Phelps of the First Baptist Church of New Haven, Conn., preaches a sermon titled "National Symptoms," in which he declares:

> A year of civil war in our country we never expected to witness. But it is now a matter of experience and history. ... we believe a New and brighter Day will spring from this National night of ours. Its symptoms already appear. Its strokes of dawn gild the horizon. The first anniversary of the war comes with events as startling as those that marked its beginning, and far more propitious. ... God signals the coming Morn by His manifest Interpositions in our behalf. ...

The morning cometh evidently, from the present aspects of the ever-perplexing Slavery question. There is now increasing hope of our ultimately becoming a free nation. ... This war, waged by its instigators in the interest of human bondage, has done more to break down that system, and thus freed more slaves in one year, than all other agencies seemed likely to accomplish in a lifetime. Indeed, slavery can never regain its former power, but must in time pass away, as utterly at variance with the fundamental principles of our Republic and the moral sense of the civilized world, and no doubt abhorrent to God, who seems to be over-ruling the wrath of man for its overthrow. ... O blessed Day of death to Treason and Slavery, come! O glorious Day of a brighter Liberty, and a freer Land, over all which the starry folds of our dear Banner shall wave in triumph and peace, come! Come, O longed-for Day of Righteousness, and thou conquering Prince of Salvation, come!

Union triumphs this month do not stop at Shiloh. Fort Pulaski on the coast of Georgia is captured by Union forces, sealing off coastal access to Savannah. Union naval forces sail up the Mississippi River and force the surrender of New Orleans. President Lincoln frees the remaining 3,500 slaves in Washington, D.C.

Yet, as the month draws to a close, white Southern Baptists are undaunted. The Georgia Baptist Convention meets and passes the following resolutions:

Resolved, That while profoundly feeling our cause is just, we nevertheless have great reason to humble ourselves before Almighty God, and to acknowledge his chastening hand in our late reverses.

Resolved, That we find in the present circumstances of the country no cause for discouragement; that God, our heavenly Father, often chastens most promptly those whom he most loves; and that, trusting in Him with the whole heart, we are more and more determined, by His blessing, to oppose the invader of our soil by ever means placed in our power and to the last extremity.

The stage is thus set for three more years of an increasingly-bloody war.

MAY 1862

White Southerners cheer as Thomas "Stonewall" Jackson troubles Union forces in Virginia's Shenandoah Valley. Jackson, while attending a Baptist congregation during his young years, came to appreciate the Bible and, in particular, studied the military actions of the Old Testament. Now, he is a warrior for God's Confederacy.

Meanwhile, Union Gen. David Hunter — from Hilton Head, S.C., overseeing the United States military presence in the Deep South — issues an order stating that persons "heretofore held as slaves, are therefore declared forever free."

U.S. President Abraham Lincoln, privately contemplating the emancipation of African slaves but sensing the time is not quite ripe, promptly rescinds Hunter's edict. Attending a Primitive Baptist church during his young years, Lincoln had been influenced by the congregation's anti-slavery stance. Now, the president awaits a more opportune time to make his own public statement. That time will come a mere four months hence.

In the Southwest, Massachusetts-born politician and Union Gen. Benjamin Butler — graduate of a Baptist college, where he studied to be a minister but instead became a lawyer — is in charge of the federal occupation of New Orleans. This month he issues an order targeted at Southern women, declaring that any woman who insults or shows contempt for any U.S. soldier or officer shall be treated as a prostitute. White Southerners do not appreciate such insolence, and give Butler the nickname, the "Beast of New Orleans."

At the same time, martial law and the suspension of the writ of *habeas corpus* in the Confederate capital of Richmond is upheld by Confederate Attorney General Thomas Watts, a prominent layman of First Baptist Church in Montgomery, Ala.

The Deep South city of Charleston this month is the site of one of the most daring events of the entire war. Slave Robert Smalls captures the Confederate gunboat *Planter* and, bringing other slaves aboard, sails past harbor defenses and behind Union naval lines. Smalls, a Baptist layman, in the months following is celebrated as a hero in the North.

Denominational writers this month are not hesitant to voice their opinions about the seemingly perilous state of the Confederacy. Samuel Boykin, editor of Georgia Baptists' *Christian Index* newspaper, offers a prescription for Southern salvation:

For the true life of a nation is its religion; and to preserve purity, sanctity, vitality in its religion, by the punishment of a nation, is the dictate of the loftiest wisdom. ... God chastises the nations of His love, lest they forget Him. ... As a people, have we not been proud, boasters, forgetful of God, seekers of pleasure, laying up for ourselves treasures on earth rather than in heaven? ... Sufficient for us is it, that our land is swept by the tornado of war; that our households are made desolate; that sorrow, suffering, want and fearful anxiety, have taken their abode near each hearth-stone beneath our fair skies. God grant that we may speedily see that it is our own sins for which we are being punished; that God is calling us out to turn from our evil ways that He may withhold His hand; and that it becomes us to repent in sack-cloth and ashes, and return to our first love, and do our first work. ... We must return to the Lord ... with renewed trust in the all-sufficing righteousness of our Redeemer. We must have more personal holiness, more zeal for good works, more liberality in Christian enterprises, more of the spirit of Christian brotherhood, and a greater regard for eternal things. ... Then will God bless us, and stay this cruel war, and change our mourning into rejoicing. Then will the Sun of His loving mercy beam forth gloriously over our land, and cause peace, prosperity and happiness, to reign supreme.

A writer in North Carolina's *Biblical Recorder* newspaper expresses gratitude that "Southern preachers," despite condemnation by Northern heretics, have "been true to the South."

They have dared to be patriotic and friends of liberty, not only in heart and sentiment, but also in word and action. With ... few exceptions ... they have stood by their country and their people through these trying times ... have not only declared the duty of Christian freeman, but shown by their example ... [and] have supported their government and their rulers.

Two worldviews are thus juxtaposed. One is hurtling toward a public political declaration that slavery is against the will of God and antithetical to just government. The other is more confident than ever that slavery is God's will for the black race, a determination so great that God himself is momentarily punishing his chosen nation to forever secure the enslavement of black persons. In this latter world view, blessed are the white ministers of the Southern gospel who remain faithful to the mission of God's Confederacy.

JUNE 1862

In an effort to capture the Confederate capital, Union Gen. George McClellan in his Peninsula Campaign continues a slow and halting march to Richmond, only to be outmaneuvered by Confederate Gen. Robert E. Lee by the end of the month. McClellan's retreat spares Richmond for now, while the successes of Lee and Gen. Thomas "Stonewall" Jackson further elevate the generals as heroes of the South.

One of the Southern successes of the Peninsula Campaign this month is the Battle of Seven Pines in Henrico County. Yet the ebullition of victory is mixed with the bitter sorrow of death. A Confederate Baptist soldier thus describes the scene near Richmond following Seven Pines:

> The road was thronged with carriages of every kind bearing off the dead and wounded while the "crash of resounding arms" saluted our ears just ahead of us. Men with wounds, the most ghastly lay agonizing in their blood, piles of human limbs lay by the road side, where the surgeons were at work. The scene beggars description, and made the blood almost curdle in our veins to witness such horrid suffering of our fellow soldiers. But there were some things that relieved these sad reflections; All along the road, squads of miserable looking Yankees were driven along at the point of the bayonet, going to Richmond — not as they expected. Many wagon loads of the spoils from the enemy — fine rifles, ammunition, elegant ambulances, (quite a number,) tents, provisions, &c., joined in the throng and cheered our boys greatly.

On both sides, battlefield casualties and deaths from wounds and illnesses rapidly mount. In addition, soldiers sometimes face danger in places unexpected, such as this incident in Richmond:

> A soldier took shelter in the portico of the First Baptist Church on Saturday, during the rain, and placed his gun against one of the pillars. Shortly afterward, by some accident, the weapon was knocked down, and exploding, lodged the ball in his shoulder. An army surgeon passing at the time rendered the necessary assistance. The wound inflicted upon the unfortunate soldier was very severe.

Increasingly, Baptist church buildings near the front lines are pressed into service as Confederate hospitals. One example is the Scottsville Baptist Church of Virginia. Taken over by the Confederacy, the church building receives its first soldier patients this month. Church members are forced to worship elsewhere during the 16 months the building is utilized by the Confederate Army.

Confiscation of church buildings by the Union Army is also commonplace. The Shiloh Baptist Church of Washington, D.C., an African congregation, temporarily loses the use of its facilities as the Union army converts the building into a hospital in advance of an attack upon Fredericksburg, Va., planned for later this year. On the other hand, church membership swells with freed slaves from D.C. and Union-occupied areas in nearby Virginia towns and cities.

Northward, members of the Third Baptist Church in Stonington, Conn., an African congregation, reflect on the war thus far:

> We are not indifferent spectators of the dreadful strife now raging in our country. ... Two of our members were for many years slaves. Though denied the privilege to enter the army to fight, we will pay our taxes when demanded. ...

Later, in the final year of war, they also declare that "whenever we are permitted to vote, we shall be sure not to vote for bondage or oppression in any form. ... We have a destiny in common with all the sons and daughters of Africa which we are bound to fulfill."

Thus, as the war enters its second summer, white Baptists remain hopelessly divided North and South, while black Baptists throughout the broken land are united in fervent hope for freedom.

JULY 1862

For the first time in months, the residents of the Confederate capital of Richmond breathe a sigh of relief. Thanks to the determined efforts of Confederate Gen. Robert E. Lee's Army of Northern Virginia, Union Gen. George B. McClellan's Army of the Potomac is driven away from Richmond in a series of battles known as the Seven Days Battles. The darkest hours of the Confederacy to date are now past. Union hopes for a quick end to the war are dashed.

J.D. Hufham, editor of North Carolina Baptists' *Biblical Recorder*, expresses his relief that the "Great Battle" has, for now, saved Richmond and the Confederacy:

> What the effects of this battle will be on the Northern people, it is impossible to foresee. It is hoped that they will gather lessons of wisdom from this disaster; that they will learn the impossibility of subjugating us and be willing to let us alone.

Many Northern Baptists, however, believe the balance of the war is on the side of the Union. The editor of the *Watchman and Examiner*, the Baptist newspaper of New England Baptists, summarizes the sentiments held by many of his fellow Northern Baptists:

> The flag of the Union floats in every rebel State. The Mississippi is lost to the Confederacy, and all the cities on its banks are at the mercy of our gunboats. Mobile, Savannah, Charleston and Wilmington are the only seaports now open to them, and these can be taken at any moment, when the plans of the campaign, formed at Washington, render it expedient or desirable.

Yet for many Southern Baptists, the most disappointing aspect of their Confederate nation remains: the evil evidenced in army life. Now fully engaged in distributing Bibles and other religious literature to soldiers, they eagerly look for any signs that their efforts are leading to the salvation of lost or straying souls. A report delivered to delegates at the annual gathering of the South Carolina Baptist Convention, a letter from an army colporteur, offers hope:

> The soldiers do not wait for me to go among them to distribute, but they crowd around my tent by scores, asking for something to read. They receive and read

with eagerness. I require them to read and return, and take others, which they do punctually. I am much pleased with the work of a COLPORTER. I had no idea it was so pleasant an employment. ... I have supplied two regiments from North Carolina. Soldiers read with eagerness and seeming delight the tracts and books which I am almost daily placing in their hands. I have just conversed with a Lieutenant, who, I fear, is on his death-bed, but who is rejoicing in hope of eternal life through a pardoning Redeemer.

Other Baptists of the South are inclined to publicly ignore the sins of their nation's soldiers, focusing instead on the widespread belief (among white Baptists) that the Confederacy is God's earthly vessel chosen to defend the rightness of African slavery. The Middle District Baptist Association of Virginia sums up such sentiments rather neatly: "If a people drew the sword in behalf of a just cause, we are that people."

In the midst of the shifting winds of the war, U.S. President Abraham Lincoln reveals a critical decision on July 22, informing his chief advisors and cabinet that he will soon issue a proclamation to free slaves. The timing is crucial. In order to lend credibility to the coming public announcement, Lincoln declares that he will wait until the Union Army achieves a notable battlefield victory.

In reality, emancipation of slaves has been underway for months. The U.S. Congress has passed two confiscation acts legally empowering the Union Army to free the slaves of persons deemed as traitors to the United States, under which thousands of slaves throughout the South have already been liberated. Yet, when Lincoln's formal Emancipation Proclamation comes, it will strike a psychological blow to the very life and vitality of the slave-based Confederacy that many white Southern Baptists view as wrapped in the mantle of God's providence.

AUGUST 1862

The spirits of the Confederacy are running high. Richmond, the Confederate capital, is safe. Generals Robert E. Lee and Stonewall Jackson are outfoxing their Northern counterparts. Conscription is swelling the ranks of the Confederate army. Inflation is a problem, but politicians, preachers, writers and the slaveholding elite are proclaiming the gospel of self-sufficiency, insisting that the South can endure long enough to tire the Northern public of the war and turn the North against its tyrannical "black president" (Abraham Lincoln).

Northward, the District of Columbia is wary of a possible Confederate offensive. The public patience is wearing thin for want of battlefield successes. In addition, many Northerners are upset over Lincoln's reticence in emancipating African slaves. Although he knows that freeing the slaves is the key to victory, and longs to announce his emancipation plan (but waiting for the most opportune moment), Lincoln's public response this month is: "If I could save the Union without freeing any slave I would do it, and if I could do so by freeing all the slaves I would do it."

Baptists, meanwhile, struggle to keep their focus on missions in the midst of the war. Especially in the Southern states, the number of active pastors and missionaries, as well as baptisms, has plunged since the beginning of the great conflict. A statement from Kentucky's Campbell County Association of Baptists reflects a common lamentation among many Baptists of the South:

> ... the idea that a financial crisis or national troubles should be an excuse
> for Christians not endeavoring to have the gospel preached is too glaring an
> absurdity to be entertained for one moment

Yet, the Kingdom of God is expanding in ways anew, enabled by the slow but steady advance of the United States military along the Southern coastline.

Hilton Head, S.C., now in Union hands, was one of the wealthiest Southern coastal towns prior to the war. Previously home to several millionaires (most millionaires in the United States before the war were large-scale Southern planters) in one of the nation's richest states, Hilton Head is now headquarters for the South Atlantic Blockading Squadron, overseeing the blockade of Savannah. Whereas the town's former millionaires made their fortunes in cotton from forced slave labor, the Union blockade of the Southern coast has made cotton worthless. In addition, under the Union policy of seizing "contraband" (a United States military term referring to slaves) of Southerners who oppose the North, Africans on the island are now freemen, some among the first to serve as black Union troops, albeit unauthorized.

Against this backdrop, the first African Baptist Church of Hilton Head is established on Aug. 17. *The New South Newspaper*, a local Union-published paper, reports on the "organization of the First Baptist Church of Hilton Head, and the ordination of its pastor":

> These events occurred on Sunday, [August] the 17th instant, and the ceremonies attending them were conducted in a very impressive manner. The society thus established numbers about 120 members, all of whom are contrabands. Of these nearly 70 were professing Christians under the rule of their late masters, while the others have been converted and baptized since our advent among them. Abraham Murchison, a colored man in the employ of the Chief Quartermaster, has been selected as the minister to these people, and was duly installed as their pastor on the Sabbath before last. The following was the order of exercises: Ordination Sermon — Chaplain H.S. Wayland, 7th Connecticut Volunteers; charge to candidate — Chaplain W.C. Patterson, 1st Massachusetts cavalry; ordination prayer and right-hand of fellowship — Chaplain H. Hovey, Volunteer Engineers; charge to the church — Chaplain Whitehead, 97th Pennsylvania Volunteers.

The African Baptists of Hilton Head are merely one example of former slaves translating their newfound freedom into religious autonomy, and by so doing acting — to the horror of their former owners — upon Baptists' overarching founding principles: freedom of conscience and voluntary faith.

The hopes of Baptists of the South, in short, are inherently conflicted. White Baptists place their hopes of maintaining white supremacy in military generals Lee and Jackson, while African Baptists know their path to salvation is through the military might of the North. Not only are the prayers of North and South at odds with one another, but the prayers of the South itself are irreconcilable.

SEPTEMBER 1862

In and around the yard of a pacifist Baptist church, the bloodiest one-day battle in American history unfolds this month: the Battle of Antietam.

Built in 1852 by German Baptist farmers, the Dunker Church on a hill near Sharpsburg, Md., houses a peace-loving congregation of six to eight farm families. The peace, however, is shattered during morning worship service on Sept. 14, as the sounds of distant cannon fire, signaling the Battle of South Mountain, infiltrate the Baptist sanctuary. Yet, South Mountain proves only a prelude to the events of Sept. 17.

The cannon fire signals the clash of Robert E. Lee's Confederate Army of Northern Virginia against U.S. Gen. George B. McClellan's army. Having driven north onto enemy soil, Lee is living up to his growing reputation as a daring commander. In an effort to seize momentum in the war, capture much-needed supplies, foment political unrest in the North, and perhaps bring Maryland into the Confederacy, Lee has forced the Union onto the defensive. McClellan proves his mettle with a victory at South Mountain, but Lee is ever resourceful as he maneuvers away and seeks high ground.

The 17th dawns shrouded in fog. Anticipation and fear hang thick in the air. Lee commands the high ground surrounding the German Baptist meeting house. McClellan is nearby. In the murkiness, a chorus of rifle fire begins. Over the next seven hours, Union forces thrice attack the entrenched Confederate forces. Stretched but not broken, the Confederate lines hold their ground. Near the end of the day the armies disengage, rifle and cannon fire fall silent, and a truce is called on church grounds. The casualties are epic: Of the 100,000 soldiers engaged in war this day, 23,000 — nearly one in four — are either dead, wounded or missing. Of those, 2,100 Union soldiers are dead and 1,550 Confederate soldiers rise no more.

The Confederate Army turns the German Baptist church into a hospital. On the 18th both armies gather their wounded and bury their dead. That evening, Lee withdraws his army across the Potomac River and begins the march back to Virginia. Upon the departure of the armies, the German Baptist church stands riddled with bullet holes and damaged by cannon fire, war having left its mark upon the pacifist place of worship. Nearly two years will pass before the building is restored.

Yet the Union victory on the grounds of the pacifist Baptist meeting house has monumental repercussions. The hopes of the Northern public are suddenly lifted. Just as importantly, the successful repulsion of the Rebel invaders provides U.S. President Abraham Lincoln the public goodwill necessary to announce his preliminary Emancipation Proclamation — long contemplated — on Sept. 22. The proclamation is to become law on Jan. 1.

Thus, Lee's Northern invasion, rather than boosting the prospects of the South, shifts momentum to the North and sets the stage for the biggest blow yet to African slavery.

Eight days after Antietam, the president jots down his evolving thoughts on Providence and war, words that are forever immortalized:

> The will of God prevails. In great contests each party claims to act in accordance with the will of God. Both may be, and one must be, wrong. God cannot be for and against the same thing at the same time. In the present civil war it is quite possible that God's purpose is something different from the purpose of either party; and yet the human instrumentalities, working just as they do, are of the best adaptation to effect his purpose. I am almost ready to say that this is probably true; that God wills this contest, and wills that it shall not end yet. By his mere great power on the minds of the now contestants, he could have either saved or destroyed the Union without a human contest. Yet the contest began. And, having begun, he could give the final victory to either side any day. Yet the contest proceeds.

Union victory in the Battle of Antietam shifted momentum to the North and paved the way for the Emancipation Proclamation. Photo by Bruce Gourley.

As the weather cools and the leaves turn color, the war grinds on. Confederate Gen. Robert E. Lee and his Army of Northern Virginia, following an unsuccessful invasion of Maryland last month, have retreated to the South. This month's primary battlefield action does not involve Lee.

The United States wins the Battle of Corinth (Mississippi) in the Western Theater and achieves a strategic victory in the Battle of Perryville in Kentucky (the largest battle fought in the state), gaining control of the Border State. Bringing cheer to the South, the Confederate Army wins several small skirmishes on their home turf, while Confederate Gen. J.E.B. Stuart pulls off a daring and successful, albeit brief, cavalry raid into Maryland and Pennsylvania. Neither the North nor the South can claim a clear upper hand over the other.

While the war is far from over, the dynamics of African slavery — the cause of the great conflict — are even now dramatically changing. Maryland, although a slave state, emphatically rejected Lee's overtures during the recent invasion, despite strong pro-slavery Southern Baptist influence in Baltimore (Richard Fuller, pastor of the city's Seventh Baptist Church, is president of the Southern Baptist Convention). Northern hero Robert Smalls, the former slave who five months earlier captured a Confederate gunboat, tours New York, speaking to large crowds and raising support for the Union. Smalls is a member of the First African Baptist Church of Union-controlled Beaufort, S.C. Another former slave, Sandy Alexander from Virginia, D.C., this month establishes the First Baptist Church of Georgetown (D.C.), not far from the former (and infamous) slave auction district in the nation's capital.

With the march to formal emancipation of all slaves now underway, Northern white Baptists on the home front do their part to support the United States Army. This month in Maine, Portland's Free Street Baptist Church, following the leadership of two widows, establishes the Maine Camp Hospital Association. Harriet Eaton and Elizabeth Fogg become part of a 21,000 force of Northern women — including many Baptists — who assist in the domestic and administrative work of Union military hospitals throughout the remainder of the war.

Within the Confederacy, some white Southern Baptist elites now find themselves in disagreement over laws prohibiting slaves from reading. While the evil writings of abolitionists Harriet Beecher Stowe and Horace Greeley sometimes yet crop up in the South, access to the Bible, these Baptists of the South argue, is a God-given right. Just as importantly, reading God's Word would help African slaves understand that bondage is God's will for the black race, thus making life easier for slaveowners by instilling happiness, morality, industriousness and "soul" eternity among the South's "servile class." These unrealistic assumptions ignore the biblical underpinnings of the abolitionist movement, while overlooking thousands of slave desertions in Union-controlled areas of the Confederacy. That no former slave wishes to return to a life of bondage is an unspoken reality.

For their part, common white home-front Baptists of the South live with anxiety and worry. Savannah's First Baptist Church hosts the Ladies Christian Association for a day of knitting clothes for "our suffering army." Ebenezer Association Baptists of Georgia lament the lack of "religious influence" and prevalence of "vice" within the Confederate Army, echoing a common theme among home-front Southern Baptists. Baptists of Alabama's Cahaba Association spend time "in prayer to Almighty God in behalf of the Army of the Confederate States of America ... praying to our Father in Heaven in behalf of our bleeding country."

As the month of October ebbs, the future of the two Americas is far from clear. The only clarity in the 18-month-old Civil War thus far is the overwhelming desire of African slaves for freedom, a point recognized by the North but denied by the South. The resolution of these conflicting narratives of freedom is the key to ending the war. But thus far, the end is nowhere in sight.

This Dunker Church, a German Baptist congregation, stood in the center of the fighting at Antietam in September 1862. Photo from the Library of Congress.

No major battles take place this month. Lincoln's Republican Party suffers losses in mid-term elections, an outcome attributed to the president's plans for emancipating African slaves. Not all Northerners are yet prepared to give freedom to blacks.

Undeterred, Lincoln declares: "We, even we here, hold the power and bear the responsibility. In giving freedom to the slave we assure freedom to the free … The way is plain, peaceful, generous, just — a way which if followed the world will forever applaud and God must forever bless."

Baptists of the North publicly voice their approval of Lincoln's course of action. The Pennsylvania Baptist Convention declares:

> That as the institution of slavery stands before the world as the confessed feeding source of the present mighty and wicked rebellion against our national Constitution, we most heartily approve of the President's proclamation of emancipation, without modification in substance and without change of time in its execution.

Many other Baptists of the North, assembled in both associational and state meetings, also voice affirmation of Lincoln's Emancipation Proclamation, invoking freedom for all persons as the will of God. On the other hand, some Northern Baptists do not view black citizens as equals.

A pending lawsuit in New York City involves the Madison Avenue Baptist Church, in which a member sues the church for refusing to finalize the "conveyance of a pew" (the practice of purchasing the annual right to sit in a given pew is a means of revenue for many churches). The church's defense is that the plaintiff "had caused a disturbance in the church by the introduction of negroes into the pew."

In the Confederacy, Pastor J. Lansing Burrows of the First Baptist Church of Richmond, Va., chairs a committee "to raise money to purchase shoes" for soldiers in General Lee's army who lack adequate clothing and footwear for the coming winter.

The annual holiday of a November Thanksgiving will not begin until next year, but this year the Union army, along with many Northern states and cities, celebrate a day of Thanksgiving on Nov. 27. Many Northerners may not yet fully embrace emancipation, but most are thankful that the tide is turning in favor of the Union in the war against the South. And with the turning of the tide, freedom for blacks yet enslaved draws ever nearer.

Unidentified Union soldiers pose in a studio. Photo from the Library of Congress.

DECEMBER 1862

This month opens with U.S. President Abraham Lincoln reiterating his commitment, in the State of the Union address, to the emancipation of Confederate slaves. Many Northern Baptists support the president. Although many Democrats agitate against emancipation and for an end to the war, Republican support ensures the president's agenda remains on track.

In addition, two major battles with differing outcomes take place this month. In the first, Confederate Gen. Robert E. Lee crushes an offensive by U.S. Gen. Ambrose Burnside in the Battle of Fredericksburg (Va.). Several Baptist churches suffer damage during the fighting, including the Fredericksburg Baptist Church. An eyewitness describes the scene following the battle:

> There is scarcely a house in the town that has not some mark of the siege. Chimneys knocked off, roofs torn up, and walls scarred with holes of various sizes, some as large as a man's head and others as large as a flour barrel. The large tall houses suffered more than the low buildings. A large Baptist Church [Fredericksburg Baptist Church] has fifteen large holes through the walls, four through the steeple and the roof torn up in many places. I think there are twenty five or thirty houses burned.

On the last day of the month, the Battle of Stone's River (or Second Murfreesboro) in middle Tennessee begins. The Union ultimately wins the battle, but at a great cost. Both sides suffer the highest percentage of casualties of any Civil War battle. Out of about 75,000 troops total, there are nearly 24,000 casualties.

While battlefield deaths mount, the Southern Baptist Foreign Mission Board in Richmond, suffering from economic recession and the federal blockade of Confederate ports, is shuttered. In response, Richard Fuller, Baltimore pastor and former SBC president, establishes a provisional mission board in the Maryland city, allowing some communication with missionaries.

In the place of foreign mission work, Southern Baptists for the remainder of the war focus primarily on Confederate soldiers. Many Baptist leaders are concerned that the Southern Army is godless and a hotbed of sin, yet their calls for army ministers often fall upon deaf ears. Of the Baptist pastors who do serve as army chaplains and missionaries, the tasks are almost overwhelming: evangelize the hundreds of thousands of heathens, reclaim backsliding church members, provide religious sanctioning of the killing of enemy soldiers, and in the face of death offer assurances of heaven to soldiers who have claimed the name of Jesus.

If mission work remains the heartbeat of Southern Baptists, state and regional newspapers serve as the public face of Baptists in the Confederacy. Such periodicals, typically published weekly, focus on Bible lessons, doctrine, Christian advice, associational and state meetings, church revivals, the Confederacy and the war. War hardships, however, have already led to the closure of several publications. This month, the *Mississippi Baptist* becomes the latest Baptist newspaper of the South to fold up shop.

Not yet celebrated as a national holiday nor in Baptist churches, Christmas Day is far from festive this year. The Lincolns visit wounded Union soldiers. In Kentucky, Confederate Gen. John Hunt Morgan makes a Christmas raid into Kentucky, destroying 35 miles of railroad track in an attempt to thwart Union advances. In the army camps of both Americas, some regiments celebrate Christmas, while others do not. North and South, many wives and children spend the day longing for their husbands and fathers.

Against the backdrop of political intrigue, bloody battles, Baptist struggles in the South and empty chairs on both home fronts, the last day of the year draws to a close with growing anticipation in the hearts of African slaves. President Lincoln's Emancipation Proclamation is to come tomorrow. Many blacks free and enslaved, the former openly and the latter quietly, forsake sleep to pray and watch for the dawning of God's long-awaited deliverance.

The year draws to a close with yet another Confederate victory, this time in the Battle of Fredericksburg. Despite the victory, the Confederacy faces the new year weakened from earlier losses, especially that of the Battle of Antietam in September. Photo by Bruce Gourley.

1863

On Jan. 1, 1863, U.S. President Abraham Lincoln issued the Emancipation Proclamation, legally freeing all remaining slaves residing in non-Union controlled areas of states in rebellion against the Union. Confederates mocked the proclamation. Slaves' actual freedom could only be realized by Union victory over the South. However, the act cheered black persons everywhere and paved the way for free blacks to serve in the Union Army. Photo from Library of Congress.

JANUARY 1863

In the midst of a war vividly marked by death and destruction on a scale unprecedented in American history, Jan. 1 witnesses the most important moment yet in the great conflict — a moment not about death, but rather an affirmation of life.

On the first day of the new year and against the backdrop of growing Northern support for abolition, President Abraham Lincoln formally issues the Emancipation Proclamation, officially freeing all remaining African slaves in areas that are yet in rebellion against the federal government. Slavery, clearly understood by both the United States and the Confederate States as the one substantial issue over which the regions disagree, is an intractable divide. It is the issue over which hundreds of thousands of white men are sacrificing their lives — Southerners long committed to denying freedom to blacks, and Northerners increasingly embracing freedom for all persons.

Since October, large numbers of Northern Baptists assembled in state conventions and regional associational gatherings have voiced support for the Emancipation Proclamation. Many Baptists of the North now celebrate the enacted law as advancing God's principles of liberty and freedom.

For black Baptists, the Emancipation Proclamation is intensely personal. In the North and in Union-controlled areas of the South, many free blacks assemble expectantly in church meeting houses on New Year's Day awaiting telegraph news of the signing of the document. Afternoon passes, darkness arrives. From Boston, Frederick Douglas describes what happens next among that city's black population gathered at the Tremont Temple Baptist Church:

> Eight, nine, ten o'clock came and went, and still no word. A visible shadow seemed falling on the expecting throng, which the confident utterances of the speakers sought in vain to dispel. At last, when patience was well-nigh exhausted, and suspense was becoming agony, a man (I think was Judge Russell) with hasty step advanced through the crowd, and with a face fairly illumined with the news he bore, exclaimed in tones that thrilled all hearts, "It is coming!" "It is on the wires!" The effect of this announcement was startling beyond description, and the scene was wild and grand. Joy and gladness exhausted all forms of expression from shouts of praise, to sobs and tears. My old friend Rue, a colored preacher, a man of wonderful vocal power, expressed the heartfelt emotion of the hour, when he led all voices in

the anthem, "Sound the Loud Timbrel O'er Egypt's Dark Sea, Jehovah hath Triumphed, His People Are Free." About twelve o'clock, seeing there was no disposition to retire from the hall, which must be vacated, my friend Grimes (of blessed memory), rose and moved that the meeting adjourn to the Twelfth Baptist Church, of which he was pastor, and soon that church was packed from doors to pulpit, and this meeting did not break up till near the dawn of day. It was one of the most affecting and thrilling occasions I ever witnessed, and a worthy celebration of the first step on the part of the nation at its departure from the thraldom of ages.

As free blacks celebrate and the U.S. Army formally begins the recruitment of black soldiers, most white Southern Baptists insist that a biblical faith demands the enslavement of the African race. An editorial in North Carolina Baptists' *Biblical Recorder* this month ignores Lincoln's Emancipation Proclamation, instead heralding a great achievement for the white race — the recent and decisive Confederate victory at Fredericksburg, Va.:

The year 1862 will ever stand forth pre-eminent among the great epochs in the history of our race. To the men of the South it possesses a deeper significance, is invested with a peculiar, thrilling interest which can only pass away with their lives. It opened gloomily enough for the Southern cause, and gave no indications of the radiant glory which marked its close. All remember well its first months of darkness and depression, when our foes confident and boastful, were closing in around us, and our destruction seemed sure. ... It was a sense of darkness, of imminent peril, the most critical period in our national history. Let it not be forgotten. If [a]day of disaster should come again, let us turn to it and remember the signal deliverance which followed.

... Who could have anticipated the pleasing change? ... It has come through the blessing of God on the energy and skill of our leaders. ... Let us recognize the hand of God in all this ... and implore the continuance of His mercies to us. To Him belong the honor and the glory. ... Such are the prospects of the opening year. We hope it will be marked by triumphs as glorious as those which have already attended our efforts to establish our independence, and have won for us the admiration of the world.

Thus, black freedmen celebrate as never before — and black slaves dare hope that their liberation is nigh — while at the same time white Southerners rejoice in battlefield victories for white supremacy. Both seize the mantle of liberty. Both praise the Almighty as the author of their respective salvation.

Suspended precariously in the middle of this epic struggle is freedom itself. Yet only one God can prevail: either the creator of a new future envisioned by an enslaved people and their Northern allies, or the lord of a dark past to which white Southerners are fiercely devoted. For Baptists, the dividing line runs right through the Bible. Southern biblical conservatism is firmly rooted in America's racist past, while a future of racial equality hinges upon a newer understanding of scriptural interpretation unfettered by the chains of biblical literalism.

Wilder Brigade Monument, commonly known as "Wilder Tower," at Chickamauga.
Photo by John Pierce.

FEBRUARY 1863

The course of the war is now clear: Whereas virtually everyone North and South from the beginning of the great conflict acknowledged African slavery as the war's cause, the United States is now on record as fighting for the cause of freedom for blacks. On the other end of the spectrum, the Confederacy ignores Abraham Lincoln's legal emancipation of Southern slaves and trumpets white liberty and black bondage as the Revolutionary War heritage to which they alone are truly committed.

Voices North and South appropriate God and Bible for their respective freedom agendas, resulting in ever more politicized sermons. While anti-Confederacy views are rarely openly expressed in Southern Baptist congregations, dissenting voices are not uncommon in the North. This month, a member of the First Baptist Church of Canton, Ohio, is dismissed for his "differences of opinion" with other members regarding the war.

Despite the cold weather, the armies of the United States maintain pressure upon the South. Against the backdrop of minimal military activity in the heart of winter, Murfreesboro, Tenn., is now under Union control, while federal troops utilize the First Baptist Church of Nashville as a Union hospital. In the winter camps Union generals address the problem of desertions by constructing better winter huts, improving medical care, and including fresh fruits and vegetables with rations. In addition, a conscription act is passed.

Economically, the U.S. passes the National Currency Act to help finance the war, while currency in the Confederacy falls to a mere 20 percent of what it was at the beginning of the war. Against the backdrop of runaway inflation, Southern Baptist newspapers routinely rail against extortion as the national sin of the Confederate States.

Meanwhile, Southern Baptist attempts to evangelize Confederate soldiers are gaining traction. In their winter camps soldiers are a captive audience, even as Southern Baptists' missionary efforts are now almost exclusively funneled toward the troops. The growing angst and escalating death count brought about by the brutal war prey upon the minds and souls of soldiers, turning the thoughts of many to the prospects of their afterlife.

J.J. Hyman, Baptist minister and soldier and chaplain in the 49th Georgia Regiment, offers his account of the moving of the Spirit among the troops:

Finding that we had gone into winter quarters, I commenced preaching regularly three times a week to each regiment in the brigade. About the 1st of February, 1863, the good Lord poured out His Spirit upon us; hundreds were seeking the Lord for pardon of sins; almost daily there were some going down into the water, being buried with Christ in baptism.

An assistant surgeon in the 1st Georgia Confederate, on the other hand, offers a rather different view of a Baptist chaplain serving at Camp Cummings near Mobile, Ala.:

In one respect I don't like our present Camp as well as the first one. We are four miles from the City. Most too far for Church + I don't go so often. There is an ignorant conceited old Baptist brother who acts as Chaplain to the Battalion. He rants + foams + murders grammar at a terrible rate every Sunday. He has the characteristic unctions, [?] appearance, manners + language that I admired so much in the association that dined at your Fathers soon after we were married. He is a good meaning old man though + I have no doubt Suits the congregation much better than [some] would.

New spiritual beginnings also take place apart from the Confederate camps. Last month's Emancipation Proclamation, understood by both free and enslaved blacks as their Exodus moment, brings about a revival in black Baptist life of the North. Established churches grow and new congregations are birthed. One of the new black Baptist congregations born this month is the Second Baptist Church of Burlington, N.J., organized by former black members of the biracial First Baptist Church of that city.

The spirits of both white and black are thus on the ascendancy. While the Confederate army is on the cusp of what will be viewed as a time of great spiritual revival, black Baptists' journey from the biblical Egypt to the promised land will yet be long and arduous.

MARCH 1863

As winter gives way to warmer temperatures and longer days, generals plot strategies and restless soldiers pack up winter quarters and prepare for impending battles.

United States military forces, determined to control the Western Theater of war, continue a slow but relentless drive to Vicksburg, a strategic city on the banks of the Mississippi River. Further to the West, Union soldiers in the Battle of Glorieta Pass thwart Confederate attempts to conquer New Mexico.

In the heart of the Confederacy, Southern forces on the defensive successfully engage Union troops in several minor battles. The Confederate capital of Richmond, safe for now, is a bustle of activity. As war causalities have mounted, many hospitals for soldiers have been established in the city, including a Baptist hospital, of which a news reporter speaks glowingly:

> The hospitals of Richmond are many of them models of comfort and cleanliness, and their good management is due to the untiring energy and administrative capacity of the noble women of our city, ladies of gentle birth and high culture who are proud to give their time to the holy work, and who ask no earthly remuneration, whose reward will be on high. ... Colonel P.W. Alexander ... testifies to the admirable routine of the hospital kept in the Baptist Institute building under the matronly superintendence of Mrs. Lewis N. Webb, of Richmond.

Also headquartered in Richmond is the Southern Baptist Foreign Mission Board, now cut off from its missionaries due to the Union blockade of the Southern coast. A provisional mission board office operating out of Maryland has found but little success, so this month the FMB hires blockade-runners, an expensive, risky and largely futile endeavor.

Further to the South, Atlanta is a busy commercial center of the Confederacy. As in Richmond, Baptists are a significant presence. A news correspondent this month describes the First Baptist Church of Atlanta:

> Decidedly the best filled pulpit in Atlanta is the Baptist, a very pretty church, under the pastoral charge of the Rev. Dr. Brantly, a son of the loved minister of the First Baptist Church in Charleston. All who listen to his terse and well-written sermons come away well pleased, and weekly crowds attest his popularity.

Along the coast, Sylvanus Landrum, pastor of the First Baptist Church of Savannah, praises his congregation's efforts in support of the Confederacy.

... there are, beside the regular Sabbath services, a prayer meeting on Tuesday afternoon, and a lecture on Thursday evening at 7 ¾ o'clock. At all our meetings soldiers are ever welcome. Then, the Board of Baptist Missions have two missionaries here, whose whole time is devoted to the religious interests of the soldiers, Rev. D.G. Daniell, long and well known in Georgia as a pastor and agent, and recently a chaplain of the 29th Regiment, and Rev. A.D. Cohen, formerly a pastor at Newbern, N C., but driven from his home by the enemy, and recently a chaplain in the Army of the Potomac. These ministers of experience, intelligence and unquestioned piety, devote their time to preaching in the camp and hospitals, and distributing tracts, hymn books and Testaments. They have circulated thousands and tens of thousands of pages of printed truth.

Meanwhile, slaves — many of whom are Baptists — are escaping from bondage in increasing numbers near areas controlled by the Union army. Baptist freedmen are now serving in black Union regiments as both soldiers and chaplains.

Competing views of the Christian faith are hardening all the more South and North. While white Southerners seemingly exhibit more zeal in their religious sentiments, faith empowers black Baptists' determination — and that of many Northerners at large — to abolish slavery.

As the month draws to a close in a war-weary nation, U.S. President Abraham Lincoln, raised in a Calvinistic Baptist church, proclaims a national day of humiliation, fasting and prayer to be held in April. Acknowledging that blessings and punishments alike are bestowed upon nations by a sovereign God, Lincoln calls upon his fellow Americans to recognize that victory lies beyond self-reliance, concluding that "It behooves us, then, to humble ourselves before the offended Power, to confess our national sins, and to pray for clemency and forgiveness."

APRIL 1863

The arrival of spring signals the resumption of military activity and an increase in homeless and hungry, poor white, home-front citizens of the Confederacy.

Warfare is especially felt upon the oceans and rivers. Although Confederate forts repel a Union naval assault upon Charleston, a federal fleet sails past Vicksburg's batteries on the Mississippi River while suffering little damage. By the end of the month, Union Gen. Ulysses S. Grant begins landing troops near Vicksburg. A Confederate victory over federal forces at Plymouth, N.C., offers some solace for the South but cannot ameliorate the worrisome Union naval encroachments on the Mississippi.

In Union-occupied Murfreesboro, Tenn., poor white refugees from the surrounding countryside are camped out in the yard of the city's Baptist church. A local businessman, with some disdain, offers an eye-witness account:

> There is a large number of [white] country people, from different sections, that has congregated here. That is commonly called refugees, who, as a class of people, are generally a degree below the negro, but, like the negro, make their appearance. Man and woman, half clad, with a half doz tow head children, all with small bundles under their arms of old quilts and a fiew articles of clothing. Another set-a man carrying a bundle, which appears to be about the house hold for himself, wife, and three or four tow heads and a dog or two. His elbows and knees out, a seedy hat, and an apology for shoes, wife half clothed and look like she had not been near water for a month or more. Children frequently bare-footed, hair resembling porcupine quills. These motly crouds make their appearance, tell a pitiful tale, say that everything they had was taken from them. It is plainly seen, they had nothing to take.

At the same time, unrest surfaces in the Confederate capital of Richmond, Va., where famished women demand bread. Gathering at the Belvidere Hill Baptist Church to discuss food and fuel shortages, female workers in Richmond's munitions and ironworks war facilities request a meeting with the governor. Their request denied, the women begin looting food from downtown shops.

Confederate President Jefferson Davis emerges from the capitol building to address the women. Emptying his pockets of change, he tosses the coins to the angry women while the governor orders home-front guards to confront the rioters. The military threat quells the Bread Riots, but Richmond seethes with unrest for the remainder of the war.

As poor whites increasingly challenge Confederate officials, enslaved blacks grow all the bolder. Each month thousands flee captivity to freedom behind Union lines. Among those remaining, many become more assertive in their bi-racial congregations, requesting fewer restrictions in their spiritual lives. In the Van Wert Baptist Church in Georgia's Paulding County, for example, "A colored Brother, Moses, applied through Brother Heaton for permission to preach in this house, when, on motion, her consent was withheld."

In Virginia, black members of Charlottesville's First Baptist Church request permission to meet separately in the church basement and choose their own deacons and pastor. Courteous and mild in their request, they understand the delicate nature of the negotiations. Upon agreeing to be led by a white pastor, they signal continued subservience. White members vote to allow the separate meetings, but two months later black members sunder ties with the white pastor. First Baptist responds by warning the black congregation to "not place the colored brethren beyond the control of the church."

As white Baptists thus maintain control over their enslaved brothers and sisters, they do so with more elasticity as well as mounting anxiety and fear. Frequently, church houses are bases for slave patrols, home-front groups of white men tasked with policing slaves on the plantation and hunting down fugitive slaves.

On April 30, a "Day of National Humiliation, Fasting and Prayer" in the North, Daniel C. Eddy of Philadelphia's Tabernacle Baptist Church offers optimistic reflections, his sermon concluding with these words:

O, what a country ours will be when the States shall be reunited; when the dear old flag wave from Maine to Georgia, from the Atlantic to the Pacific; when slavery shall have become extinct; when the barbarism of Southern society shall have given way to a better civilization; when those immense cotton fields shall be worked by free labor, or cut up into farms for our brave soldiers; when by those blood-dyed rivers shall rise huge manufactories; when there shall be no cause of desolation and strife, but when all will be animated by a common faith in Liberty and Religion! That day will come. It may be away over some dark trials, beyond fearful calamities, but it will come. It will be such a day as Washington and Hancock and Adams pictured and dreamed about, and prayed for. It will come with blessings, and be greeted with Hallelujahs, it will be the Millennium of political glory, the Sabbath of Liberty, the Jubilee of Humanity.

This month opens with Confederate Gen. Robert E. Lee achieving the high point of his war-time battlefield successes by overcoming long odds and soundly defeating Union forces in the seven-day Battle of Chancellorsville, Va. In the middle of the fighting of May 3 stands the Salem Baptist Church. Damaged, the small brick building nonetheless survives.

Confederate victory, however, comes at a terrible cost. Thirty-nine-year-old Confederate Gen. Thomas "Stonewall" Jackson, widely recognized among Southern Baptists as an exemplary Christian leader, dies on March 10 from complications after having been accidentally shot by friendly fire at Chancellorsville.

As Jackson lies upon his death bed, the Southern Baptist Convention convenes in Augusta, Ga. The assembled delegates are a who's who of prominent Southern Baptist pastors and denominational leaders, most of whom are slaveholders.

The home missions report focuses heavily on the need for more army missionaries. Delegates also form a committee "to report suitable resolutions to be adopted by the Convention in regard to the war now raging in this country." One of the seven resolutions declares:

> The war which has been forced upon us is, on our part, just and necessary, and have only strengthened our opposition to a reunion with the United States on any terms whatever … we have no thought of ever yielding, but will render a hearty support to the Confederate Government.

Another resolution acknowledges "the hand of God" upon the Confederacy, noting "we confidently anticipate ultimate success."

One resolution acknowledges sins for which repentance is needed, but excludes African slavery, the very issue over which the war is being fought. Other resolutions call for evangelization of soldiers, sympathies and help for families displaced by war, and diligence to the moral and religious training of children in the face of the war. The final resolution addresses the death of Jackson:

That we have just heard with unutterable grief, of the death of that noble Christian warrior, Lt. Gen. T.J. Jackson; that we thank God for the good he has achieved, and the glorious example he has left us, and pray that we may all learn to trust, as he trusted, in the Lord alone.

Northward, the American (Northern) Baptist Missionary Union convenes at Cleveland, Ohio, presided over by U.S. Senator Ira Harris (N.Y.), a leading Baptist layman of the North. Like their Southern counterparts, delegates pass resolutions concerning the war. One resolution condemns "the authors, aiders, and abettors of this slaveholders' rebellion, in their desperate efforts to nationalize the institution of slavery and to extend its despotic sway throughout the land." Another resolution states:

That in the recent acts of Congress, abolishing slavery forever in the District of Columbia and the Territories, and in the noble proclamation of the President of the United States, declaring freedom to the slave in States in rebellion, we see cause for congratulation and joy, and we think we behold the dawn of that glorious day when, as in Israel's ancient jubilee, "liberty shall be proclaimed throughout all the land, until all the inhabitants thereof.—Leviticus xxv.10."

Thus heroes both are the recently deceased General Jackson and President Lincoln, respective to Baptists South and North. While having little in common ideologically in regards to the war, both men trace their spiritual roots to the respective Baptist congregations of their boyhoods.

The other significant battlefield action this month takes place in the Western Theater of war on the Mississippi River. U.S. Gen. Ulysses S. Grant, following months of preparation, wins several significant victories in the area of Vicksburg, Miss., a fortified Confederate city that the United States considers essential to gaining control of the Mississippi River and dividing the Confederacy East and West. Following the battlefield victories, Grant sets siege to the city on May 22.

As the month draws to a close, sadness and apprehension pervade the Confederacy. Jackson is dead and Vicksburg under siege.

Conversely, United States politicians and the general public, following the unfolding saga on the Mississippi River, desperately hope that Grant will be able to turn the tide of the war in favor of the North.

JUNE 1863

Hoping to gain a military advantage and foment unrest in the United States near the end of this month, Confederate Gen. Robert E. Lee leads his army from Virginia into the North for a second time. While Lee's forces invade Maryland and then Pennsylvania, the Union Army scrambles to respond.

At the same time, U.S. Gen. Ulysses S. Grant is deep in Southern territory, besieging Vicksburg, Miss. Control of the Western theatre of war rests upon taking the river city. As weeks pass and supplies in the city run low, many trapped Confederate soldiers and citizens alike fall victim to hunger, despair, disease and death.

As spring gives way to summer, Baptists in annual gatherings South and North offer support for their respective nations and armies.

Virginia Baptists reaffirm the Confederacy as God's chosen nation and African slavery as God's will for blacks:

> ... we are daily more convinced of the righteousness of our cause, and have abiding faith, through His favor, of ultimate, and we trust not distant deliverance from our ruthless enemy. We are contending not only for political liberty, but for rights of conscience, assailed by fanaticism in the name of religion. ...

> ... those [Northern Christians] who claim to be the followers of the meek and lowly Jesus — ministers of the reconciliation — heralds of the gospel of peace, have sown the seeds of the whirlwind which is devastating the land. It is now many years since our Northern brethren, in their fierce hostility to the institution of domestic slavery, deaf alike to the voice of reason and the authority of Scripture, to the pleadings of patriotism and the claims of Christian charity, by their fiery and intolerant fanaticism furrowed deep and broad the line of separation — thrusting us from their communion as unworthy to labor with them in the fields of Christian benevolence and gospel enterprise.

In the North, Illinois Baptists condemn slavery:

> We cordially support the [Lincoln] administration in their efforts to put down the rebellion, and hail with joy the proclamation of emancipation, believing that when we as a nation shall "keep the fast which God hath chosen" "that our light shall break forth as the morning, and our health shall spring forth speedily."

We recognize human slavery now, as we have heretofore done, to be the cause of the war and its kindred evils, and we reiterate our convictions that there can be no peace and prosperity in the nation until it is destroyed. We feel that the hope of our country in the suppression of treason in the revolted States, and in our midst, lies not merely in military successes or in military orders, but in the incorruptible virtue and the profound devotion of the people to the principles of the glorious gospel of the blessed God.

Free Will Baptists in the North express their ardent desire for the "everlasting overthrow of the accursed institution of American slavery":

The system of slavery in this land has received its death-blow. The wound can never be healed. This is generally admitted on all sides. No compromise will ever be made between the North and the South, to restore this God abhorred system to its former position. It may be months, and even years, before it entirely expires. There may yet be severe struggles and mighty death throes, but die it must and die it will; and may God hasten the happy day.

Meanwhile, former slave and abolitionist Harriet Tubman guides Union soldiers on raids in the upper reaches of South Carolina's coastal rivers. The campaign results in the freeing of some 750 slaves who are transported to the Baptist church of nearby Union-controlled Beaufort before being resettled as free persons. More Union raids into the countryside follow, further loosening the grip of slaveowners in the region.

The month of June thus closes with each nation's army standing on enemy ground. Apprehension is high North and South as the war over slavery hangs in the balance.

For a few brief days, the hopes of the Confederacy soar as Gen. Robert E. Lee's Army of North Virginia invades the North. Early in the morning of July 1, advancing Confederate forces enter Gettysburg, Penn., expecting no resistance. To their surprise, they encounter two Union cavalry brigades. Fierce fighting ensues, the original brigades on both sides reinforced throughout the day with newly-arriving soldiers.

For most of the day, Gen. Abner Doubleday — from a Baptist family and considered by some as the inventor of baseball — is the ranking Union commander. On the Confederate side, Lee arrives mid-afternoon.

The Rebels slowly drive federal forces back, and by nightfall Union troops are fortified atop Cemetery Hill and Ridge southeast of the town, while Confederates claim high ground a mile to the west and north.

On July 2 the Confederates launch an unsuccessful attack on Union lines. The following day at 2 p.m., Lee orders an assault on the Union center on Cemetery Ridge. Fifteen thousand Rebel soldiers march across a mile of open field and are decimated by Union artillery. A few breach the enemy's line, but are soon forced to retreat in what becomes a decisive Union victory.

The costliest battle of the war is effectively over. Lee suffers his first major battlefield loss. Some 51,000 are dead, wounded, missing or captured, including one-third of Lee's army. Gettysburg proves to be the major turning point of the war.

As the remnants of Lee's army retreat southward on July 4, a second staggering blow to the Confederacy comes as the Southern stronghold of Vicksburg surrenders to Union forces following weeks of besiegement. Driven from the North and now divided East and West, despondency settles over the Confederacy and is reflected in the lamentations voiced in many Baptist churches of the South.

Yet while dented, public faith in the Confederacy seemingly remains firm. Three days after Gettysburg, the Elon Baptist Church of Virginia's Dover Association declares that Christians must "aid and encourage them [Confederate government officials] in every effort to secure our social and religious freedom" and resolves:

That the war which the U. S. government has forced upon us, involving as it does, our social and religious freedom, must be met with unfaltering determination and earnest cooperation of every Christian.

"Social freedom" refers to the racial arrangement of black slavery and white supremacy, of which white Baptists of the South give little indication of surrendering.

On the other hand, Mary Beckley Bristow, a Kentucky Baptist and Confederate sympathizer, voices both the despair and remaining hope of many other Baptists of the South:

This very circumstance so painfully [occur]ing to me and ten-thousands of others of the oppressed and down trodden South may be for the benefit of our people in the All-powerful hands of Almighty God, as impossible as it seems to us short-sighted mortals.

Northward, the victory at Gettysburg, while cheered, leads to a need for more soldiers. Drafts enacted in New York City lead to three days of rioting as mostly working-class Irishmen protest the common practice of wealthy Northern men paying a $300 commutation fee to avoid enlistment.

Another notable clash this month is the Battle of Fort Wagner on South Carolina's Morris Island, a daring Union assault led by an African-American regiment against a coastal Confederate fort.

The Massachusetts 54th Regiment, the first black army unit raised in the North, attacks the heavily-manned outpost on July 18. In the heat of the battle the flag guard is wounded. Baptist and former slave William Carney seizes the flag, holding it high amid the fierce, bloody battle. Badly wounded, Carney crawls forward to the parapets of Fort Wagner, planting Old Glory in the sand.

Although the Confederates win the battle against a vastly outgunned foe, the bravery of the 54th Massachusetts shows the world that black troops can fight valiantly against overwhelming odds. (The story of this battle, with Hollywood liberties, is told in the movie *Glory*.)

The month of July thus reconfigures, but does not end, the war. Confederate hopes are dimmed, yet a dogged determination remains. The will of U.S. civilians is tested despite major battlefield victories. And the valor of free black soldiers points the way to a new source of military reinforcements in the North.

AUGUST 1863

Following Union victories in the battles of Gettysburg and Vicksburg in July, Confederate Gen. Robert E. Lee tenders his resignation to President Jefferson Davis, who refuses the offer. Discouragement and disillusionment settle over the South, mixed with a determination on the part of many soldiers and citizens to fight to the end.

In the North, the victory over Lee leads citizens, soldiers and politicians to anticipate a quick resolution to the war. A national day of thanksgiving is filled with sermons and speeches rejoicing that black slavery is almost banished and victory over the South is at hand. One such discourse is delivered in the Baptist church of Brookline, Mass., by John D. Murdock, who near the conclusion declares:

> It is the glory of our National Constitution that it bases itself on the sacred rights of human nature. It recognizes the divine foreordination of freedom for all men. Chief among its objects was to promote the general welfare, and to secure the blessings of freedom to posterity. And though it has been perverted and thwarted by men whose aims were alien to its spirit, it has at last been wrested from their hands, and freedom is now proclaimed under the broad shield of its authority, throughout all the land, to all the inhabitants thereof. Hitherto its exceptions have been exalted above its leading design. Its temporary provisions have been set in opposition to its fundamental principles. But at length the exceptional wrong has given place to the essential right. If the people have only the virtue and firmness to stand upon its noble aims, and the public policy just inaugurated in pursuance of them, the clouds will soon clear away, and a new day of freedom and prosperity will dawn on the land. The Constitution shall at last be recognized as the bond, while the Flag shall be the symbol, of Universal Freedom. And out of this chaos of blood and strife a new order of equality and justice shall emerge, and the rejoicings of the free shall be like the song of the sons of the morning in the dawn of creation.

In no mood for celebration, the Confederate nation observes a day of fasting. Southern Baptist divine I.T. Tichenor delivers the fast day message before the Alabama legislature, in which he laments:

Two weary years of war have wrung this question from the agonized heart of our bleeding country. "Oh! That we could have peace!" exclaims the statesman, as he ponders the problems that demand solution at his hands. "Peace," sighs the soldier, as he wraps his blanket around him and lies down to sleep upon the open field. "Peace!" moans the widow, as she reads the fatal news of her heroic husband fallen on some bloody field, and bitterly thinks of the darkened future in store for herself and her orphaned children. The prayer of the land is for peace. You may hear it in the sanctuary, at the fireside, around the family altar, in the silent chamber, on the tented field. When will it come?

Tichenor goes on to express his confidence that God is on the side of the slave-based Confederacy:

If God governs the world, then his hand is in this war in which we are engaged. It matters not that the wickedness of man brought it upon us, that it was caused by the mad attempts of fanaticism to deprive us of our rights, overthrow our institutions, and impose upon us a yoke which, as freemen, we had resolved never to bear.

Amid the animated discourse, little formal military action takes place this month. But far to the West, Quantrill's Raiders, a band of Southern guerrillas, attack Lawrence, Kan., and kill some 183 men before burning the town. On Quantrill's hit list is Jacob Ulrich, a German Baptist minister, and Abraham Rothrock, an elder in Ulrich's church. Neighbors, the two men are prominent abolitionists. Warned of the impending attack, Ulrich and his family flee and hide in the nearby woods, as does Rothrock. The raiders set the Ulrichs' house and barn on fire, but the family saves the house once the men ride away.

Union forces retaliate by evacuating Confederate-sympathizing citizens out of four Missouri counties and burning homes, barns and crops.

In an ominous sign for the Confederacy at large, black soldiers are entering Union army ranks in droves. The American Baptist Missionary Convention seeks U.S. President Abraham Lincoln's permission to send black Baptist chaplains among black soldiers. Lincoln replies that their "object is a worthy one, and I shall be glad for all facilities to be afforded them which may not be inconsistent with or a hindrance to our military operations."

This month thus sets the contours of the second half of the war: A confident Union presses a withering but defiant Confederacy, both sides certain of God's favor, while U.S. army ranks swell with soldiers of the very race that the South is determined to keep enslaved in perpetuity.

SEPTEMBER 1863

This month in Tennessee, Union forces occupy Knoxville, seize the Cumberland Gap and take Chattanooga in rapid succession and with few casualties. Yet the advance comes to a sudden and bloody standstill when Confederates win the Battle of Chickamauga in the greatest Union defeat in the war's Western Theater, totaling some 34,000 casualties, second only to Gettysburg. Despite the victory, Confederate losses are greater than those of the Union. Retreating to Chattanooga, the federals retrench for more battles that are sure to come.

Meanwhile, earlier Confederate losses at Gettysburg and Vicksburg have led to unprecedented revivals among soldiers and on the home front. Southern Baptist newspapers routinely report mass conversions, yet largely ignore growing army desertions. In associational gatherings throughout the South, army mission work is highlighted and defiant support of the Confederacy voiced.

An editorial in the North Carolina Baptist *Biblical Recorder* echoes sentiments publicly voiced among white Baptists:

> Our reverses are not ruinous. They are what must be looked for in a war of such magnitude. And if rightly received, they will be among the most powerful agencies for good to the nation. ...What we shall gain by this war will be blood-bought; and so sacred will be these treasures, that the people of the confederacy must ever cherish and defend them next to their religion. Every man, not now fit to be a slave, must place a proper estimate on these rights and blessings for which we contend; and must ask, in all the fervor of his patriotism give me a place where I can aid in achieving the independence of this land. And, having found his place, he must stay there and labor, and suffer, and be hopeful, and wait for deliverance that a just God will bring to a Christian people struggling to be free.

A Confederate Baptist mother in Kentucky, however, writing in her diary, is not fully persuaded by such lofty rhetoric:

> The South has had many reverses and to me, a short sighted worm of the dust, those late reverses look almost irreparable. Yet I know in the hands of an Omnipotent God those very things that make my heart sink and flesh cringe may ultimately prove the best things that could have happened for the cause I deeply & devotedly cling to. I have also been anxious, O, so very anxious,

to hear from our darling boy far away in the Confederate army. ... Now I feel so anxious to know how that sickness terminated, where he is, & what he is doing. O, would it please God to guard & guide our loved one, shield him from disease & death in battle, and bring him safely home to us at the right time, if it be His sovereign will. And if it be decreed that we should see that manly form and dear face no more on earth, may it be Thy will we should meet in that bright, glorious world, where wars cannot come, where sickness and sorrow, pain nor death are felt nor heard no more.

Within the United States, the Erie Baptist Association of New York convenes and, offering sentiments similar to other Northern associations, passes resolutions of loyalty to the Union and support of freedom for slaves. The latter resolution states:

Resolved, That we have special occasion for thankfulness to God, in the emancipation last January, of nearly three millions of our fellow men from bondage, and still another such occasion in our recent National victories.

Hundreds of thousands of blacks yet enslaved grow more hopeful, while freed persons exercise their newfound autonomy. The African-American Baptist congregation in Union-occupied Port Royal, S.C., holds a special event to raise funds for the creation of a monument to Col. Robert Shaw, commander of the 54th Massachusetts African Regiment killed in action in July. In Washington, D.C., 21 black Baptists, now free but exiled from their home in Fredericksburg, Va., establish the Shiloh Baptist Church.

Late summer and early fall thus witness the now-weary tale of battlefields strewn with bodies. Yet the war is increasingly transformed apart from the battlefield by defiant white Southern men and despondent white Southern women, Confederate army revivals and desertions, ebullient Northern civilians and growing political will, and hopeful slaves and autonomous free blacks.

Appeals to God and providence aside, final triumph, dark and distant, demands human determination.

OCTOBER 1863

Chattanooga is the major focus of the war this month as the Union solidifies control of the city and environs against the backdrop of quarrels among opposing Confederate officers.

Apart from the fighting, Southern Baptist news editors and pastors sing the praises of the revivals occurring within the Confederate Army. The Central Baptist Association of Alabama's Coosa County meets and, like many other Baptist associations of the South this fall, affirms army missionary work:

.... great good has been, and is now being accomplished through the labors of our missionaries and colporteurs in the armies of the Confederate States in awakening our noble soldiers to their great spiritual interests, and enabling them to enlist in the service of the King Emmanuel ...

Some churches hold special prayer meetings. Delegates to the Mississippi Baptist Association recommend that their churches "meet on the first Lord's day in every month at ten o'clock to offer up special prayer for the success of our cause and the spiritual welfare of our enemies."

In North Carolina the United Baptist Association endorses "the cause of the Southern confederacy" and condemns soldier desertion.

God is also on the mind of the Northern public. U.S. President Abraham Lincoln issues a Thanksgiving Proclamation to be observed on Nov. 26:

I do therefore invite my fellow citizens in every part of the United States, and also those who are at sea and those who are sojourning in foreign lands, to set apart and observe the last Thursday of November next, as a day of Thanksgiving and Praise to our beneficent Father who dwelleth in the Heavens. And I recommend to them that while offering up the ascriptions justly due to Him for such singular deliverances and blessings, they do also, with humble penitence for our national perverseness and disobedience, commend to His tender care all those who have become widows, orphans, mourners or sufferers in the lamentable civil strife in which we are unavoidably engaged, and fervently implore the interposition of the Almighty Hand to heal the wounds of the nation and to restore it as soon as may be consistent with the Divine purposes to the full enjoyment of peace, harmony, tranquility and Union.

The proclamation, the beginning of an annual Thanksgiving observance, is embraced by many Northern congregations. Pennsylvania Baptists pass the following resolution:

Whereas, Our national Government grew out of Baptist polity, exemplified by men of whom Roger Williams was the type at the North, and a little Baptist church near the residence of Thomas Jefferson, from whom he declared he obtained his first ideas of Republican Government, was the type at the South:

Resolved, That we should be derelict to our principles as Baptists, and unworthy sons of worthy sires, if, in this crisis in our existence, we withheld our support, influence, and sympathy from our Government.

2. That it is our duty, both as citizens and Christians, to speak boldly our sentiments with regard to the causes of the existing rebellion, that ministers should speak boldly on the subject, and that those who take offence at such utterances are unworthy of a place in the Christian church.

3. That we, the members of this Convention, as patriots, as Baptists, and as Christians, do express our unqualified support of our National and State Governments, in their efforts to suppress the present rebellion.

4. That we have occasion for gratitude, that not only the full apostolic proportion of eleven-twelfths of the Christian ministry among us are truly loyal Government supporters, but that the mass of the piety of our churches and the intelligence of our country occupy the same position.

5. That the recent victories at the ballot-box should be accepted with thanksgiving to God, as exhibiting the loyalty of the people, and as an evidence of the continued blessing of God on us as a nation.

6. That in the President's Proclamation of Emancipation, made valid by the exigency which called it forth, and in his recent declaration to abide by it, we see the progress of Christ's kingdom, which will proclaim liberty to all the earth.

7. That we urge the churches throughout the Commonwealth to observe the last Thursday In November next, according to the recommendation of the President, as a day of public Thanksgiving to God.

NOVEMBER 1863

Lamenting over lives lost and dwelling upon the themes of sacrifice, redemption and higher purpose, President Abraham Lincoln gives a two-minute speech that is later recognized as one of the greatest addresses in American history.

Four score and seven years ago our fathers brought forth on this continent, a new nation, conceived in Liberty, and dedicated to the proposition that all men are created equal.

Now we are engaged in a great civil war, testing whether that nation, or any nation so conceived and so dedicated, can long endure. We are met on a great battle-field of that war. We have come to dedicate a portion of that field, as a final resting place for those who here gave their lives that that nation might live. It is altogether fitting and proper that we should do this.

But, in a larger sense, we can not dedicate — we can not consecrate — we can not hallow — this ground. The brave men, living and dead, who struggled here, have consecrated it, far above our poor power to add or detract. The world will little note, nor long remember what we say here, but it can never forget what they did here. It is for us the living, rather, to be dedicated here to the unfinished work which they who fought here have thus far so nobly advanced. It is rather for us to be here dedicated to the great task remaining before us — that from these honored dead we take increased devotion to that cause for which they gave the last full measure of devotion — that we here highly resolve that these dead shall not have died in vain — that this nation, under God, shall have a new birth of freedom — and that government of the people, by the people, for the people, shall not perish from the earth.

Otherwise, Chattanooga is the focus this month. Union Gen. William T. Sherman and his Army of Tennessee reinforce the besieged federals and dislodge Confederate forces holding the high ground near the Union-controlled city in a series of battles from Nov. 23-25.

The Confederates retreat across the state line to Dalton, Ga. Confederate hospitals in Dalton (including the hospital housed in the First Baptist Church), Marietta, Atlanta and Macon receive an influx of wounded soldiers. Despair again sweeps across the South. Georgia Baptists, facing the prospect of invasion by the enemy, hold days of fasting and prayer.

Following Chattanooga, slave Dick Gray, serving alongside his owner during the battle, returns to Texas with the one surviving son of his dead master. After emancipation, Gray changes his name to Richard Henry Boyd, becomes a Baptist minister, helps organize the Negro Baptist Convention of Texas, and later becomes one of the leading Baptist citizens in Nashville, Tenn.

Northward, Nov. 26 is a day of Thanksgiving as proclaimed by Lincoln. The event is the first of annual Thanksgiving observances henceforth in the United States. For the occasion, Baptist pastor I.S. Kalloch of New York City's Laight-Street Baptist Church preaches from 1 Thess. 5:18, "In every thing give thanks." His sermon declares, in part:

> Thanksgiving is a duty. Under all circumstances and in all things we are to give thanks. It is never so bad with us as it might be. It is never so bad as it would be if we had our deserts. Even in time of war, there is much to be thankful for. War, even civil war, is not the worst thing. Degradation, stupidity, the insensibility that can neither feel nor resent an injury, is as much worse than war, as war is worse than holy peace. As death is preferable to life purchased at the price of honor, so is war, in its bloodiest strides and ghastliest calamities, infinitely preferable to national peace purchased at the price of national degradation. ... Brave-hearted bleed that we may rejoice; gallant heroes fall that our liberties may stand.

In Minnesota, the first black Baptist congregation in the state, comprised of former slaves from Missouri who escaped via the Underground Railroad, acquires a meeting space and is soon accepted as a mission arm of the First Baptist Church of St. Paul.

Meanwhile, on Union-occupied Island No. 10 in the Mississippi River near Memphis, Joanna P. Moore from Illinois, with $4 in her pocket, arrives as the first American Baptist home missionary appointed to the South. Her mission field consists of "1,100 colored women and children in distress" and a Union Army encampment. Moore remains in the South for 40 years, serving as a missionary among the region's poor, destitute, and uneducated and becoming known as the "Swamp Angel of the South."

DECEMBER 1863

Winter weather limits troop movements and allows generals time to devise new tactics for future battles. This month the war is waged primarily on the home front, where imagination and memory serve in place of military strength.

Momentum is decidedly on the side of the United States. With much of the South now under Union control, Lincoln offers a proclamation of pardon outlining the basic elements of Southern reconstruction. At the same time, an uncharted, post-war future of freedom for blacks is envisioned on the grounds of a prominent former plantation.

Days after the Civil War began on April 12, 1861, U.S. Col. Robert E. Lee resigned his commission from the United States Army to cast his lot with the Confederate States of America. His decision effectively ceded the Lee plantation, Arlington Estates, to the North. Union forces occupied the estate, land inherited by Lee's wife Mary from her father and located across the Potomac River from Washington.

Arlington Estates in the months and years following became a microcosm of the unfolding narrative of the war over slavery. While fighting to preserve slavery, then-Confederate Gen. Robert E. Lee in 1862 was required by the stipulation of his father-in-law's will to free the family's remaining slaves. U.S. President Abraham Lincoln's 1862 emancipation of slaves in D.C., followed by his national Emancipation Proclamation of Jan. 1, 1863, resulted in a great influx of former slaves into the capital city. Overcrowding in the city led Lincoln to turn the Lees' plantation into a temporary camp for freedmen.

This month, Freedmen's Village is formally established at Arlington Estates, completing the ironic makeover of the plantation. Religious ceremonies and speeches by army and government officials mark the occasion. Hundreds of free black families move into their newly constructed homes and begin acquiring educational, vocational and living skills. Even though the settlement is operated under military rule, the village provides an early vision of a future of racial equality.

Religion is central to the freedom movement and the black experience. By the end of the month, a non-denominational village chapel opens for services. Yet many if not most village residents are Baptists, and the first two denominational churches constructed on village grounds are of Baptist persuasion: Mt. Zion Baptist Church and Mt. Olivet Baptist Church. Freedmen's Village is dismantled in 1900, while the Baptist congregations remain to this day.

Within the Confederate States the growing number of emancipated slaves contributes to widespread national gloominess. The second half of 1863 has been marked by major battlefield losses. Soldier deaths are rapidly mounting. Confederate soldiers are deserting in record numbers even as fresh recruits are hard to come by. Home-front families, hungry and despondent, are fomenting domestic unrest.

In desperate times true believers double down, and this is no exception. In the ideological heart of the Confederacy, the South Carolina legislature holds a day of "fasting, humiliation and prayer," reaffirming their commitment to the godly cause of African slavery and their confidence in ultimate Confederate victory.

Believers also, Baptist denominational leaders and newspaper editors of the South assure their white constituency that despite the difficult times at hand, God would ultimately lead his chosen nation to victory over the barbarous Northern abolitionist enemies.

Georgia Baptist *Christian Index* editor Samuel Boykin epitomizes the desperate hopes of a white Christian South. Dismissing the present "dark cloud," he looks to the past and writes of "a prophetic vision" of a Southern future "flecked" with "snowy" cotton where "happy negroes throng the fields" while "indulgent masters" dwell in "luxurious farm houses" and "church spires innumerable point gratefully to heaven."

Boykin's message to his white readers ends thus:

Arouse from your apathy! Cease from your money-getting! Fly to the arms and rush to the rescue! Let God and men and angels behold the terrible earnestness of your purpose to be independent! Be not dismayed by disaster; for before you lies a path of honor and renown all lit up by suns of glory. ... Arise, then, in your might, and hurl the invaders from your border, and soon shall be filled this prophetic vision.

Believers and dreamers, the past and the future thus intersect as the year draws to a close. Much has yet to transpire before the war is over, but a trajectory is emerging. Many non-combatants North and South recognize the inevitability of the outcome of the great conflict and are even now lending hands and minds to begin mending the present brokenness, a process in which reality, imagination and memory battle for the upper hand.

1864

From June through November 1863, the Union and the Confederacy battled over Chattanooga and surrounding environs, ultimately resulting in Union victory. As 1864 dawns, Union
control of Chattanooga opens the door for Union forces to drive south toward Atlanta. Pictured is the view from Point Park, a high ground during the Nov. 24, 1863 Battle for Lookout
Mountain. Photo by John Pierce.

JANUARY 1864

As harsh winter weather sets in and armies hunker down, soaring inflation cuts to the bone of the Confederacy. Food now costs almost 30 times more than in 1861.

With Confederate soldiers starving, President Jefferson Davis acquiesces to Gen. Robert E. Lee's request to commandeer food in Virginia, upsetting local citizens. Many soldiers, hungry and disheartened, desert their regiments and journey homeward.

Meanwhile, the United States experiences its own troubles. Foremost is the problem of military desertion, which reaches an all-time high. Contributing to the situation are schemes to pilfer government coffers by abusing a law allowing draftees to avoid military service by paying a fee for a substitute. Instances of disabled men being hired to replace the able-bodied soar.

Yet the Union Army maintains the upper hand in the war, and the march for freedom for slaves continues. Black congregations throughout the North and Union-controlled areas of the South celebrate the one-year anniversary of the Emancipation Proclamation. In Portsmouth, Va., seven black members withdraw from the Court Street Baptist Church and, against the wishes of white members of the church, begin holding their own worship services in a black-smith shop.

In Washington, D.C., what will become the 13th Amendment to the U.S. Constitution takes the form of a joint resolution by the Senate and House to abolish slavery nationally and permanently. Green Clay Smith, a Baptist layman and congressional representative from Kentucky, is a champion of the resolution. At the same time, President Abraham Lincoln presses forward in efforts to normalize relations with Southern states under Union control.

Lincoln's strategy of reconstruction includes religion. The U.S. Secretary of War grants American (Northern) Baptists permission to occupy abandoned Baptist pulpits in Union-controlled portions of the South. One Northern Baptist editor rejoices that "we are marching on with a tread that is shaking the very foundation of things. Hundreds of abandoned Baptist pulpits will be open to loyal Baptist Ministers of the North."

The American Baptist Home Mission Society quickly appoints J.W. Parker, a Baptist pastor in Boston, to oversee the "possession" and "occupying" and ministry of Southern churches that have been "deserted by former occupants," until which time the Confederate States are defeated and the churches are able to support themselves. To this end, the ABHMS issues a call for Northern churches "so long blessed with an able ministry" to provide their pastors with a salaried leave of four to six months to "occupy each a deserted house and gather a church from the broken fragments of society and scattered members of former churches there to be found."

White Southern Baptist leaders, not surprisingly, are outraged. Indignant that the abolitionist enemy has determined to take over their very houses of worship, some leading voices immediately decry a violation of their religious liberties. Even worse, though, is the charge — vividly expressed in editorials in Southern Baptist newspapers — that the real goal of Northern Baptists is to place black preachers in every pulpit of the South. If the goal is to alarm rank-and-file believers and elevate opposition to the North, the image of blacks serving as pastors of Southern churches probably does the trick. Surely this is the biblical abomination of desolation, a sign of the end of times, and must be resisted to the death.

Providentially, on the very day that American Baptists receive permission to occupy Southern churches, the editor of the Virginia Baptist *Religious Herald*, perhaps fearful of just such a move on the part of Northern Baptists, pens an unequivocal editorial equating abolitionism — "the humanitarianism of the age" — as the Antichrist:

> Is not the true character of this humanitarianism betrayed by the fact, that it gains currency, for the most part, in those countries, in which the divinity of Christ, and even the inspiration of the Scriptures, pass into the form of nominal beliefs, or encounter rejection as exploded superstitions?

> This seems obvious. And then, does not humanitarianism — the germ of the last and crowning mystery of iniquity — everywhere voice itself in anti-slaveryism? Is not abolitionism, therefore, (to say no more,) the point of transition, for the present age, to that "apotheosis of man" — first, of man's nature, next of individual man — which shall constitute "the final Antichrist!" And in fighting against Abolitionism are we not fighting against "the final Antichrist"?

With the rhetorical warfare escalating to new levels in the cold of winter, there seemingly can be no turning back for faithful believers of a God-ordained, biblical-mandated society of white supremacy and black slavery — even as the future of the Confederacy is at its darkest yet.

FEBRUARY 1864

Due to winter conditions, military activity is largely confined to the Deep South this month. Federal forces seize the Mississippi cities of Jackson and Meridian, as well as Jacksonville, Fla. Of little consolation to the South are Confederate victories in minor skirmishes in both states as well as at Dalton, Ga. In each instance Union forces are only temporarily stymied. In southwest Georgia, Andersonville Prison opens, a prison destined for infamy for the harsh treatment of Union captives.

Battlefield despair aside, white Southern Baptists rejoice when Confederate Gen. Robert E. Lee suspends military drills and inspections in his army during Sunday morning worship time. The order comes in the midst of ongoing revivals in the Confederate camps. Baptists of the Confederacy hope that the growing number of chapels popping up in winter camps will lead to battlefield successes in the spring and summer.

Many Southern Baptists, nonetheless, lament the acute shortage of Baptist chaplains in Confederate ranks, often chastising churches and pastors for failing to invest time and effort into evangelizing Southern soldiers. In reality, money is scarce and Baptists are the one denomination refusing government pay for military chaplains.

Somewhat perversely, the saving of souls is juxtaposed against a marked increase in the execution of Confederate deserters in an effort to stem the growing tide of desertions. Compounding the problem is the fact that U.S. President Abraham Lincoln's offer of pardon to Southerners who pledge loyalty to the Union has proven surprisingly popular in much of the South.

Especially unappreciated by white Baptists of the South are efforts by Northern Baptists to place Northern ministers in vacated Southern pulpits. "We are not conquered yet," warns one Southern Baptist editorial, referring to their Northern brethren as robbers who are not prepared to "pay the price of blood necessary to place the American Baptist Home Mission Society in possession" of Southern churches.

Southern protestations aside, the United States Congress continues inching toward the abolition of slavery nationally and permanently, of which many Baptists of the North approve. This month the Senate takes up consideration of a proposed constitutional amendment:

All persons are equal before the law, so that no person can hold another as a slave; and the Congress shall have power to make all laws necessary and proper to carry this declaration into effect everywhere in the United States.

The wording changes in the months ahead, ultimately leading to the 13th Amendment to the U.S. Constitution.

The Confederacy, however, is determined to resist emancipation. The Southern Baptist press cheers this month when Confederate President Jefferson Davis calls the war to preserve white supremacy and black slavery "our holy struggle for liberty and independence" that will be won "under Divine Providence."

Southern whites applaud when Northern prejudices against racially-mixed marriages take center stage in Washington, D.C. this month. Samuel Sullivan Cox, a Baptist layman and Democratic congressman from Ohio, accuses the Republican Party of advocating miscegenation, a practice of which Northern whites widely disapprove. The furor over mixed marriages continues into the summer, imperiling Lincoln's hope for re-election. Not until after Lincoln wins the White House for a second time in November is the miscegenation scandal proven to be a hoax perpetuated by Democratic newspapermen, of which Congressman Cox had been an unwilling dupe.

Amidst the ugliness of war and politics, beautiful things yet happen. In the North, Baptist musician William Batchelder Bradbury (author of the tunes to such popular hymns as "Jesus Loves Me," "He Leadeth Me" and "Just As I Am") meets and inspires blind poet Fanny J. Crosby to write songs. At Bradbury's insistence, Crosby writes her first song, a patriotic Civil War piece titled "There Is a Sound Among the Forest Trees." Bradbury also asks Crosby to write a hymn. In response she writes "Bright Home Above," giving it to Bradbury as a gift. Thus begins Crosby's amazing musical career, during which time she writes more than 9,000 songs.

Finally, black Baptists are no bit players in the drama this month. Thousands of black slaves escape to freedom. Many former slaves now serve in the United States Army, fighting for freedom for their yet enslaved brothers and sisters. New, free black Baptist congregations are established almost weekly, both in the North and the South.

As the winter wanes with the close of the month, the impending spring promises new advances in the march for freedom for all.

As winter slowly recedes, this month witnesses a series of strategic moves on the part of the United States. Evidencing a desire to bring the war to a quick, successful close, the U.S. Senate confirms Gen. Ulysses S. Grant as the commander of all Union forces. In addition, President Abraham Lincoln signs legislation allowing Colorado and Nevada to become states. The states' production of gold and silver is crucial to the war effort.

While the Union focuses on military leadership and financial resources, few battlefield engagements take place. A force of 500 Union cavalrymen approaches within two miles of Richmond, the Confederate capital, before being driven back. Confederate Gen. Nathan Bedford Forrest makes raids into Kentucky, capturing the city of Union. Federals strengthen their presence in Arkansas, while in Louisiana Union forces advance toward Alexandria.

In southwest Georgia, Andersonville Prison assumes full-scale operations. An open-air prison, Andersonville soon gains notoriety among Union ranks as the worst of the Confederate prisons. Sanitation is virtually non-existent. Prisoners attempting to escape are summarily shot. The tall, tight-fitted log walls of the facility allow not even a crack for viewing outside. Only the sky is visible to the prisoners, a blessing and a curse: a blessing in that a view of the heavens is at times reassuring, a curse in that the men huddled below are as imprisoned to the elements of the sky as they are within the impenetrable walls.

Many Baptists are incarcerated at Andersonville during the war. Years later, a former Baptist prisoner from the 7th Tennessee (Union) speaks of the enduring legacy of the prison:

> The end of the war did not erase the bitterness caused by the 7th Tennessee's experiences. Thirty years after the war when one of Forrest's men was called to be minister of the Bethel Baptist Church in Carroll County, one of the former prisoners at Andersonville protested. He was admonished to forgive as Jesus did. Alfred D. Bennet of Huntingdon replied "the Lord was just crucified, he never had to go to Andersonville Prison."

Currently, forgiveness is far from the hearts and minds of Confederate soldiers. A Southern Baptist army missionary from North Carolina speaks of how serving in the Confederate Army makes better Christians of men, invoking, perhaps inadvertently, Constantinian imagery:

Under the light of religion a fact has been observed now for the first time (I believe), that there is something in the stern duties of a soldier and in his perilous trials that stirs his heart to meet at once the solemn duties of religion. Hence, he, with a noble magnanimity of soul, at once rises up in moral courage to do his duty to God. What proof of the power of religion thus to enable a man to bear the cross in the army...

Northward, Baptist minister and Union soldier William Elgin views God a bit differently. The chaplain of the 14th U.S. Colored Infantry, Elgin believes God is on the side of African Americans, his will expressed in the march for freedom for Southern slaves. Stationed at Chattanooga, Elgin teaches black soldiers to read and write, in addition to the skills of soldiering.

One of thousands of slaves fleeing to freedom this month is Baptist Peter Barrow. Born into slavery near Petersburg, Va., Barrow at a young age had been taken to a plantation near Cosita, Ala. Escaping bondage behind Union lines at Vicksburg, Miss., he enlists in the 66th U.S. Colored Infantry, serving through the remainder of the war. Thereafter he becomes active in politics, in addition to co-founding the Calvary Baptist Church of Spokane, Wash., the city's first black congregation.

Also this month, North Carolina Baptist layman Jonathan R. McHargue enlists in the Union's 50th Pennsylvania Infantry. A mere six months earlier McHargue had enlisted as a Confederate soldier in the 4th North Carolina Infantry, only to be wounded and subsequently captured by Union forces. His capture appears to have been a blessing in disguise, as following his recovery the North Carolinian took an oath of amnesty and was released, after which he voluntarily enlisted in the Union Army.

Collectively, the stories of Elgin, Barrow and McHargue, representative of many thousands of other stories this month, reflect the already-doomed trajectory of the Confederate States of America. The pace of the emancipation of slaves quickens, even as more and more white Southerners, soldiers and civilians alike accept Lincoln's offer of pardon in return for pledging loyalty to the Union. God, it seems, has chosen sides, a dawning realization perhaps reflected in some Southern Baptists' growing anxieties concerning the fate of the Confederacy.

APRIL 1864

With the arrival of warmer weather, military activity and political action heat up throughout the South.

In Louisiana, the Confederates emerge victorious in the Battle of Mansfield in De Soto Parish in which the Union suffers more than 2,000 casualties, compared to about 1,000 for the Confederacy. The next day the two armies clash again, this time the Union claiming victory in the Battle of Pleasant Hill.

While battles rage, the political climate of Louisiana turns sour for the Confederacy. The state's Constitutional Convention, meeting in New Orleans, adopts a new state constitution abolishing slavery. Within days, neighboring Arkansas inaugurates a pro-Union state government in Little Rock.

News of the capitulation of Louisiana and Arkansas is met with joy by C.H. Corey, former pastor of the First Baptist Church of Seabrook, N.H., and now serving with the United States Christian Commission in Port Hudson, La. There he preaches the gospel, distributes religious reading materials and otherwise ministers to Union soldiers. After the war, Corey serves as a missionary among the freedmen.

In the Border State of Maryland, Richard Fuller, Southern-born resident of Baltimore and past president of the Southern Baptist Convention, pledges loyalty to the United States, even as he grieves over his hurting homeland.

Reconstruction thus gains steam, reinforced by U.S. Senate votes to abolish slavery and approve the 13th amendment to the U.S. Constitution.

Nonetheless, the intensity characterizing the beginning of the fourth year of war harbors heightened danger for African-American Union soldiers. Confederate forces under the command of Gen. Nathan Bedford Forrest rout Union forces at Tennessee's Fort Pillow, slaughtering a high percentage of African-American enemy soldiers. Jefferson Davis orders that any captured black soldiers who were slaves must be returned to their masters.

Revenge and executive orders aside, trouble is evident even in the Deep South. Dozens of women in Savannah, Ga. riot over the lack of food in their city. When the riots are quelled, three women are thrown into prison.

Amid the swirl of events that collectively hold little promise for the South, the Confederacy observes a national day of fasting and prayer. Many Southern Baptist congregations gather for prayer, including churches in Macon, Ga.:

The Fast Day was duly observed in Macon by all the congregations. An unusual solemnity pervaded the city, and the people repaired to their respective houses of worship and bowed humbly before God and besought his favor; and as such appears to have been the case generally throughout the country, we expect the divine blessing upon our people and upon our cause.

Throughout all of Georgia, white Baptists are concerned about the future. The annual gathering of the Georgia Baptist Convention at Atlanta's Second Baptist Church is a subdued affair. Great concern is expressed over the lack of enough Baptist army chaplains and for the growing number of orphaned children due to soldier deaths.

Regardless, evidence of "divine blessings" upon the Confederacy seemingly finds expression in revivals among soldiers and in churches, including the Union Baptist Church of Wayne County, Ga., where this month "scores of sinners presented themselves for the prayers of the church; out of which number sixty expressed an experimental knowledge of religion — twenty-five of whom have been baptized."

Recently-freed slaves in the South also enjoy blessings this month. Black Baptists in Union-occupied Nashville, Tenn. separate from the white Central Baptist Church and form their own congregation, later known as the First Baptist Church of East Nashville.

In Washington, U.S. Congressman Green Clay Smith of Kentucky, a Baptist layman, in a congressional speech offers his thoughts on the month's developments and the future of the war:

Louisiana and Arkansas are free, with free constitutions and free-State Congressmen. You have no conception of the vast numbers of men who come from those sections of the country to Washington and ask the Government to go on with this work. The majority of the people of this Commonwealth do not propose to resist the action of the Government. They do not seek to do it, for if they do they must meet the consequences. I love Kentucky, as a proud and glorious Commonwealth, but love my whole country more. She stands as a bright star in the galaxy of nations, and must not be plucked out. The time is coming, not only in Kentucky, but in every Southern State, when the dark clouds will pass away, and all be under one Administration, under one Government, under one flag, and you cannot prevent it. The hundreds of thousands who have lost their lives in the struggle have not lost them in vain.

MAY 1864

Virginia. Louisiana. Georgia. U.S. military offensives spring forward throughout the South, reaching deeper into the heart of the Confederacy and waging a contest of attrition and willpower against the numerically inferior Confederate armies.

The fiercest clashes take place in Virginia, where U.S. Gen. Ulysses S. Grant's Army of the Potomac relentlessly attacks Confederate Gen. Robert E. Lee's Army of Northern Virginia, only to be repulsed in the battles of the Wilderness and Spotsylvania Court House. Afterward, Grant and his officers sit on pews in the church yard of the Massaponax Baptist Church and plot their next move. Then on they go, doggedly pursuing and engaging Lee again the last day of the month in the beginning of the Battle of Cold Harbor.

Churches are often the casualties of army movements, as is the Enon Baptist Church of Chesterfield County, Va., which is dismantled by Union forces and the lumber appropriated for the building of a military hospital.

Confederates also score a victory in Louisiana this month, thwarting Union efforts to reinforce Alexandria. The occupying federals torch and desert the city, an event witnessed by American Baptist minister Charles H. Corey, working for the U.S. Sanitary Commission: "The city was soon wrapped in flames; houses, stores, churches, everything seemed on fire; women and children were in tears."

Yet the Union offensive in Louisiana continues, including the federals' liberation of thousands of slaves as the army marches southward from the city.

In the heart of the Confederacy the much-anticipated Atlanta Campaign begins when Union Gen. William Tecumseh Sherman moves his armies southward out of Chattanooga and into Georgia. Day after day, the Federals push southward Gen. Joseph E. Johnston's Confederate Army of the Tennessee.

Reaching Paulding County west of Atlanta on May 25, Sherman attempts to outflank Johnston but is prevented from doing so in the Battle of New Hope (Baptist) Church. Fighting takes place in the church's cemetery. The battle ends in a draw as Sherman's offensive temporarily stalls.

Northward, American Baptists gather at the First Baptist Church of Philadelphia for the 50th anniversary celebration of the American Baptist Missionary Union. Among the resolutions offered is the following:

Resolved, That we regard the rebellion inaugurated by the Southern States for the purpose of destroying the Union which our fathers founded, and establishing a slaveholders' confederacy, as utterly causeless and inexcusable — a crime against civilization, humanity, freedom, and God, unparalleled in all centuries.

An address delivered to the American Baptist Home Mission Society also speaks to slavery and abolitionism, rejoicing that "more than a million of slaves have obtained the blessed boon of freedom," while looking forward to ultimate Union victory and noting that America is a nation "in the throes of its second birth. In the hot furnace of civil war its purification is being accomplished."

U.S. President Abraham Lincoln, increasingly anxious to bring a successful conclusion to the war, receives a copy of the resolutions passed at this month's Home Mission Society gathering. He responds in writing:

... I can only thank you for thus adding to the effective and almost unanamous support which the Christian communities are so zealously giving to the country, and to liberty. Indeed it is difficult to conceive how it could be otherwise with any one professing christianity, or even having ordinary perceptions of right and wrong. To read in the Bible, as the word of God himself, that "In the sweat of thy face shalt thou eat bread,["] and to preach there — from that, "In the sweat of other mans faces shalt thou eat bread," to my mind can scarcely be reconciled with honest sincerity. When brought to my final reckoning, may I have to answer for robbing no man of his goods; yet more tolerable even this, than for robbing one of himself, and all that was his. When, a year or two ago, those professedly holy men of the South, met in the semblance of prayer and devotion, and, in the name of Him who said "As ye would all men should do unto you, do ye even so unto them" appealed to the christian world to aid them in doing to a whole race of men, as they would have no man do unto themselves, to my thinking, they contemned and insulted God and His church, far more than did Satan when he tempted the Saviour with the Kingdoms of the earth. The devils attempt was no more false, and far less hypocritical. But let me forbear, remembering it is also written "Judge not, lest ye be judged."

JUNE 1864

Fierce battles and tense politics mark the month of June. The Union strategy focuses on wearing down the inferior Confederate armies and taking Richmond and Atlanta. Wearied and depleted Confederate forces hope to halt the enemy's advance long enough to stir up a political backlash against Abraham Lincoln in the North.

Ten miles from Richmond in the Battle of Cold Harbor, one of the bloodiest and most lopsided battles of the war, Confederate Gen. Robert E. Lee secures what will prove to be his last victory. Fighting in the battle is Col. Jeremiah C. Drake, formerly pastor of the Westfield Baptist Church, New York, and now commander of the 112th New York. Raked by enemy fire, Drake suffers fatal injuries. His last words are: "Give my love to my wife. Tell my friends and tell my countrymen I die a brave man, I die at peace with the world, and I trust at peace with my God."

Union Gen. Ulysses S. Grant accepts defeat but does not give up. Retreating from Cold Harbor, Grant lays siege to Petersburg, a major supply center for Richmond. Lee quickly digs in nearby. Grant's strategy of choking off Richmond before a final assault marks a worrisome turn for the Confederacy. The capital city cannot survive without Petersburg. Lee had earlier predicted that should the federals lay siege to Petersburg, it would be "a mere question of time" before the Union won the war. Lincoln, realizing the stakes, visits Grant's entrenched army this month.

In Georgia, Union Gen. William T. Sherman, slowly advancing toward Atlanta, continues pressuring Confederate Gen. Joe Johnston's Rebel forces. A series of maneuvers and battles takes place in which Sherman's forces are victorious, including the Battle of Gilgal Primitive Baptist Church, where the log meeting house is destroyed. Shortly thereafter the Confederates score a much-needed, if temporary, victory at the Battle of Kennesaw Mountain.

While battles take place in other states, their significance pales to the action in Virginia and Georgia.

On the political front, Lincoln is re-nominated as the Republican Party's presidential candidate, with Andrew Johnson of Tennessee as the vice-presidential nominee. Believing that the United States will win the war, Lincoln perceives Tennessee to be critical to reconstruction efforts.

Baptists of the Shiawassee Baptist Association in Michigan meet and offer sentiments reflective of most Baptists of the North:

Resolved, That we deeply sympathize with our Government in its efforts to suppress this rebellion, and will ever aid her to the best of our ability, with our lives, our property, our counsels and our prayers.

Resolved, That as human slavery is a sin and an abomination in the sight of God — a terrible misery and disaster to man, and wholly inconsistent with the teaching of the word of God, and opposed to the genius and spirit of our institutions; therefore we do most earnestly hope and pray that when God, in His providence, shall remove the portentious clouds of war now darkening and desolating our land, no relic, except the lifeless and horrid remains of that institution, shall be found on any part of the soil of these United States of America.

For more than three years now, many Northern Baptists have been praying for victory over the rebellious Confederacy and for an end to slavery, while many white Baptists of the South have offered prayers to the contrary.

While the prayers of the latter remain unchanged in substance, the petitions are growing ever more intense. That the Confederacy is outmanned and outgunned is obvious to all. Samuel Boykin of the Georgia Baptist *Christian Index* repeats yet again a mantra affirming God's favoritism upon the slave-based Confederacy:

The Lord Almighty alone can give us victory, and he alone can make our victories prove blessings to our country. Let us confess and forsake our sins, and turn to the Lord with all our hearts. Then we can say in pious faith, "The Lord is my strength and my shield; my heart trusteth in Him, and I am helped, and therefore my heart rejoiceth, and with my song I will praise Him."

As always, black slavery is not thought to be a sin, nor is the blessed institution to be forsaken. But by now, many white Southern plain folk have their doubts about fighting to preserve the wealth of the nation's elites.

JULY 1864

Although June's victory in the Battle of Cold Harbor offered a brief reprise, the ill fortunes of the Confederacy are now in a free fall. The tenuous nature of the South is such that the Confederacy offers to negotiate for peace in Canada. Negotiations do take place, but Confederate officials refuse Lincoln's conditions of restoring the Union and abolishing black slavery.

Meanwhile, Confederate Gen. Jubal Early, trying to relieve pressure on the Southern capital of Richmond, attempts an unsuccessful invasion of Washington, D.C. In Georgia, Confederate forces, for more than two months pressed ever further southward toward Atlanta, are defeated on July 22 in the Battle of Atlanta near Decatur. The city does not fall at this time, but it now appears inevitable that Atlanta will be captured by Union forces.

At the same time, the Battle of Petersburg continues as Union forces attempt to cut Richmond's supply lines. The battle is so spread out that some soldiers do not know how the fighting is going. Thomas Cheney of the First New Hampshire Voluntary Light Battery and a member of the First Free Baptist Church, Manchester, N.H., writes his brother, revealing how little he knows:

> ... up around the City of Petersburg there is almost continual fireing, and Occasionaly it is very heavey, what it is for or what is being done there I have to get from the Papers the same as you do.

As the Confederacy reels from setback following setback, Lincoln and the United States are growing increasingly confident that victory is inevitable. Amid growing optimism, the U.S. repeals the 1850 Fugitive Slave Act that mandated the return of escaped slaves to their masters and had remained in effect for slaves of Union loyalists in the Border States.

Most white Baptists of the South, however, still refuse to acknowledge the wrongfulness of black slavery. Focusing on spirituality rather than social justice, Texas Baptists celebrate the ecumenical work of one of their own, army missionary W.A. Mason, as reported in one newspaper:

> Elder Mason has also organized the "Christian Association of Waterhouse's Brigade," composed of the members of the different denominations, who, laying aside all sectarian prejudices, have convened at the altar to worship God, and do all they can for the promotion of the much neglected cause of

Christ. Committees are appointed from the different regiments, whose duties are to visit the sick and procure every possible comfort for them.

South Carolina Baptists also celebrate the successes, and acknowledge the challenges, of Baptist army missions:

> We have found that the more our brethren have gone among these men, the more they are anxious to preach to them the saving truths of the Gospel. They find among them the same classes we have at home — the young and the old, the learned and the unlearned, the good and the bad. Here are the same hard-hearted, careless, godless sinners, who care neither for God nor regard man, who profane His holy name, who violate His Sabbaths, who despise His laws, and who count even the blood of Christ an unholy thing, and trample His grace and offers of mercy under their feet. And the number of these is not small. Let those who think that our armies are all, or nearly all, converted to God, go among them in their regiments, or along our public highway, and they will soon be convinced that, notwithstanding so much has been done, there remains yet much, very much more, to be done.

Southern white piousness aside, the thousands of former slaves who are Baptists and are now wearing the Union blue know that spirituality and the gospel cannot be detached from human freedom. In Virginia and Georgia and beyond they fight for freedom for all blacks, enjoying the support of most white Baptists of the North. At the same time, freed persons of Baptist faith on the home front relish and celebrate freedom of worship in a revival atmosphere, their congregations growing and prospering in Union-controlled areas of the South.

The Fourth of July serves as a snapshot of racial and regional Baptist moods this month. While free black Baptists join Baptists of the North at large in enthusiastic celebration of the holiday, most of their white Baptist counterparts in the South have little interest in observing the anniversary of the U.S. Declaration of Independence, a document that long ago declared "all men are created equal."

AUGUST 1864

This month is marked by a string of United States victories over the reeling Confederacy. Most notable is the Union's rousing naval triumph in Alabama's Mobile Bay early in the month, a victory that provides a badly-needed boost to U.S. President Abraham Lincoln's re-election campaign.

As if on cue, the fall of Mobile Bay presages further Union successes, including in the Atlanta Campaign. By the end of the month, Union forces arrayed against Atlanta have driven as far south as Jonesboro, severely disrupting Rebel supply lines and overwhelming Confederate defenders. The fall of the key Southern city is mere days away.

Nonetheless, a brief and brilliant ray of hope shines across the South land this month. On the afternoon of Aug. 21 in what becomes known as the Second Battle of Memphis, Confederate raider Maj. Gen. Nathan Bedford Forrest and 2,000 cavalry temporarily occupy and cause havoc in Memphis, Tenn. Forrest withdraws after a glorious two hours, taking prisoners and supplies with him.

Forrest's Memphis raid aside, some Southern Baptists in the trenches reflect this month upon a cruel war seemingly without end. Hosea Garrett of Co. G, 10th Texas Infantry, engaged in the defense of Atlanta, writes to his uncle, Hosea Garrett Sr., in Chappell Hill, Texas. Garrett Sr., a prominent Texas Baptist and president of the Baptist General Convention of Texas, is one of the richest plantation owners in Washington County, Texas.

> We are all quite tired of this war. ... I can't believe that God will let such a people [Northern soldiers] go unpunished. I believe that the day for their overthrow is not far distant. I have heard that they cut the throat of a very wounded man that they came across in Miss. ... And I heard that some of our men found some of their wives tied to stakes and dead from the cruel treatment that they received from their foul hands. If such as this will not make men desperate, what will? We are not what we should be in a religious point of view, but I am certain that we have no soldier that would commit such outrageous acts on helpless women and children as theirs has been guilty of. I would to God that our entire Amy were true Christians. ... Pray the Lord to spare me though this cruel war, and that I may do some good in the name of my master's cause. I have tried to make a Christian soldier as well as a soldier for my country's rights. In this I pray to be sustained.

Garrett is among many white Southern Baptists, whether soldiers or ministers or lay leaders, who remain firmly committed to the Confederacy's "rights" of white supremacy and black slavery. Not a few are quite public in their sentiments, their diatribes not infrequently criticizing Baptists of the United States for pandering to Lincoln's abolitionist despotism.

Among the Southern Baptist churches in the Confederacy unshuttered from the ravages of war, national anxieties hover ever close. In revival meetings, religious conversions offer some relief from hardships. Funds for army missions are a staple of associational gatherings. A Virginia Baptist layman charges that apart from the pulpit, his state's clergy talk only of the war and the Confederacy. In other pulpits, the war mingles with the Gospels. North Carolina Baptists lament the loss of many ministers who have been killed in the great conflict, while most Baptist pastors in Middle Georgia reject calls to minister to soldiers, choosing instead to remain in their pulpits.

Enslaved Baptists, sitting in the galleries of white-led congregations, remain silent but attentive in the presence of white Baptists, a quietness belying their faith in an abolitionist God of whom Lincoln is the new Moses chosen to lead God's people to freedom.

For their part, Northern (American) Baptists believe defenders of black slavery to be cruel and unbiblical. In sermons and writings they decry slavery and rejoice that the evil practice will cease when the Confederacy is defeated. One such sermon this month, preached at the white Lima Baptist Church in New York, celebrates "the freedom and divinity of man" and "the glorious claims of human brotherhood." New black Baptist congregations in the North and Union-controlled areas of the South celebrate both freedom and brotherhood.

The decades-old competing Baptist claims for the moral high ground on the issue of black slavery have changed not a bit. But the course of the war over slavery has shifted, and reality is pointing toward a victory for those yet living in bondage.

SEPTEMBER 1864

The fall of Atlanta to Union armies on Sept. 2 dominates this month's storyline. Confederate Gen. John Bell Hood, unable to prevent Union Gen. William T. Sherman's advance upon Atlanta, abandons the city, but not before ordering the burning of all military supplies and installations. The city is aflame as Sherman's troops march in.

Upon occupying Atlanta, Sherman sends a message to U.S. President Abraham Lincoln announcing that "Atlanta is ours, and fairly won." Slaves remaining in the city welcome their newfound freedom, while white civilians are soon ordered to leave their homes. Columns of refugees flow southward by rail, horse, wagon, and carriage and on foot. Many of Atlanta's white Baptists relocate to Macon and, in the weeks and months to come, worship in the city's First Baptist Church, joining other Atlantans who previously fled to Macon.

Following the capture of Atlanta, Abraham Lincoln pens a letter to Eliza Gurney, a Quaker widow, in which his words echo his Baptist Calvinist rearing:

> The purposes of the Almighty are perfect, and must prevail, though we erring mortals may fail to accurately perceive them in advance. We hoped for a happy termination of this terrible war long before this; but God knows best, and has ruled otherwise. We shall yet acknowledge His wisdom and our own error therein. Meanwhile we must work earnestly in the best light He gives us, trusting that so working still conduces to the great ends He ordains. Surely He intends some great good to follow this mighty convulsion, which no mortal could make, and no mortal could stay.

So significant is the capture of Atlanta that President Lincoln sets aside Sept. 5 as a national day of celebration in the United States. The victory ultimately assures Lincoln's re-election in the November presidential election.

The harsh blow to the Confederacy in Georgia is followed by setbacks for the South in Virginia. The soldiers in Confederate Gen. Robert E. Lee's Army of Northern Virginia, by now having defended Petersburg for months in trench warfare, are growing desperate. Food supplies run out mid-month. Fortunately, a successful raid to capture nearby cattle provides temporary relief. On the other hand, Confederate forces are driven out of the Shenandoah Valley, after which Union troops destroy the region's crops to further deprive Lee's army of food.

Late in the month Union Gen. Ulysses S. Grant begins an offensive to breach Confederate lines at Petersburg and assault Richmond. Grant gains ground, but Lee successfully counter-attacks, temporarily holding back the tide. The inevitable, however, has been set in motion. It is only a matter of time before Richmond, the Confederate capital, falls to the enemy.

As the North celebrates the capture of Atlanta and Lee worries about the fate of Richmond, a routine notice of a runaway slave appears in the *Richmond Daily Dispatch*, an ordinary offer of a reward that hints of the resistance of the city's black Baptist community to slavery and white supremacy:

> Two hundred and Fifty dollars Reward for my Servant, Edward, twenty or twenty-one years old, black, stout and likely; has a scar near or upon one ear; is a good house servant. He left my farm on Sunday night, the 28th ultimo, and is, I believe, in Richmond, where he has relatives and friends. He may possibly be found at the African Church, or other meetings of Baptist negroes.

Even as clear heads North and South realize the end of black slavery is near, a desperate slaveholding culture, reflected among Southern Baptist leaders, clings with determined ferocity to the religiously-fueled certainty that liberty is for whites only. One Southern Baptist editor this month, echoing decades of Southern Baptist pro-slavery rhetoric, condemns the abolitionist "Yankee nation" as "blinded by fanaticism and infidelity" in their attempts to destroy the South's slave-based way of life.

Even as the Confederacy is collapsing, able-bodied white men are bound by duty to resist the invading Northern hordes. Readers of Southern Baptist newspapers this month are again reminded that deserters from the Confederate Army are ungodly traitors deserving of death.

On the home front, Baptist associational meetings throughout the Confederacy this month reflect a weariness of the war. In such gatherings, many white Baptists remain defiant, some by now have lapsed into silence, and others fear — whether openly or quietly — that the war is lost.

Conversely, the future for black Americans in the South, Baptists included, is looking brighter with each passing day.

OCTOBER 1864

With the United States Army now in control of the Southern city of Atlanta, Confederate forces led by Gen. John Bell Hood vainly try to disrupt Union supply lines. Failing, Hood attempts to lure Union Gen. William T. Sherman out of Atlanta to Alabama on terrain favorable to the Rebels.

Undeterred, Sherman is busy devising a large scale march to the Georgia coast and then northward. The general is ready for "hard war," the kind that will demoralize home-front Southerners and pressure remaining Confederate armies.

While Sherman plots and the Confederacy loses numerous small battles, Mary Beckley Bristow from Kentucky laments the war's effects upon her life. She yet wants to believe that the Confederacy will somehow prevail.

> I have spent a great deal of my life and all of my money raising negroes for old Lincoln to take from me at his pleasure. But the truth is, and I know it is strange but true, that although I and two of my brothers will be left dependent or nearly so if our negroes are taken, yet I cannot care about it. The idea of losing our independence as a nation and having the Abolitionists to lord it over us is what seems unbearable and causes a perfect writhing of my heart strings. I am certain the Lord will let our enemies go so far and no farther than he pleases.

The institution of black slavery, however, remains the declared will of God. Throughout the Confederacy, many white Baptists are certain that personal sins are responsible for the ill fortunes of their beloved nation. The South will yet be saved if white citizens evidence more piety, repent of greed or attend the Sabbath regularly.

Evidencing a small dose of humanity toward slaves, the Georgia Baptist Association meets and passes a resolution of protest against state laws that prohibit slave marriages. Other Baptist associations in Georgia also adopt the resolution.

Not so fast, say Baptists of the North. Neither personal religion nor petitions to allow slaves to marry will suffice. Slavery is inherently sinful and must be abolished. As have countless Northern Baptists previously, the Philadelphia Baptist Association blames slavery as the cause of the war:

... slavery (never to be justified by the mild, temporary, patriarchal servitude of the Old Testament), the enormity and brutality of which has few parallels in the history of ages, lies at the basis of the wicked attempt to overthrow the Government, is responsible for the bloodshed and crime of the past three years, and should be held accountable before God and man for every life sacrificed and every drop of blood shed ... no permanent peace, no lasting Union, and no public safety can be expected while slavery exists; and as an outlaw upon civilization, a pirate on human rights, the foe of God and man, alike the enemy of the white and black, it should be utterly, immediately, unconditionally and eternally blotted out, as one of the foulest stains that ever rested upon any civilized land ... the only road to peace, and the only hope of Union, lie in the subjugation of the rebellion, the extermination of its cause, and the overthrow of its supporters; and therefore, until the necessity ceases, we should welcome taxation, sacrifice, and if needful, universal conscription — our motto being "First Christ's, then our country's!"

Philadelphia Baptists, voicing their "unswerving loyalty" to the United States government, condemn the treasonous South and pledge to "crush the rebellion and restore the unity of the States." Should the Confederacy perish, "their blood will be upon their own heads."

Despite having conquered Atlanta, wresting the "foulest stain" of black slavery from the clutches of the South's biblically-certain white supremacists, and thus bringing an end to the war, remains a daunting task that may require the extreme sacrifices noted by Philadelphia Baptists. Yet one giant hurdle must first be surmounted: Abraham Lincoln, the one U.S. presidential candidate firmly committed to ending slavery at all costs, must first be re-elected in November.

The outcome of the looming presidential election, however, is far from assured.

NOVEMBER 1864

One of the most pivotal moments of the war takes place this month with the re-election of U.S. President Abraham Lincoln. With Lincoln's victory, the prosecution of the war against the rebellious Southern states continues unabated. While Southern political and religious leaders remain defiant, the odds that the Union will emerge victorious over the Confederacy have never been better.

George Dana Boardman, pastor of the First Baptist Church of Philadelphia, preaches a sermon this month declaring that the U.S. government, in its devotion to freedom and liberty for all, is divinely ordained. His is one of hundreds of similar sermons delivered during the war thus far.

New Jersey Baptists voice similar feelings, while also declaring that "since the war into which we have been forced is essentially a conflict between freedom and slavery, we see no method of terminating this conflict, and desire no other, than by the utter extinction of the system of slavery throughout all the national territory."

Meanwhile in the Confederate capital of Richmond, gang warfare — a wartime problem involving boys mired in poverty and seeped in racial hatred — breaks out near the Second Baptist Church of Richmond, as reported in the *Richmond Sentinel*:

> Emmett Ruffin and Thos. S. Dodge were yesterday evening arrested, by officers Chalkley and Griffin, on 6th street, near the Second Baptist Church, while with a good many other boys, they were engaged in a rock battle with some "basin cats." None of the "basin cats" were arrested, as they fled to their fastnesses on the approach of the officers.

> This practice of throwing stones in the streets has become an intolerable public grievance. — Every evening a crowd of boys collect on Navy Hill, and, with slings, stone every negro that passes within two hundred yards of them. We expect to hear of some of the negroes being killed, as even a very small boy can throw a stone from a sling with sufficient force to break the adamantine skull of a negro.

In central Georgia, legions of makeshift hospitals house many thousands of wounded and ill Confederate soldiers. Many of the hospitals are housed in churches, including the First Baptist Church of Griffin.

Some congregations, such as the First Baptist Church of Macon, hold overflowing worship services filled with local members along with Baptist refugees from the Atlanta area.

Also in Georgia, a new war tactic is unveiled. Union Gen. William T. Sherman's army of 62,000 troops on Nov. 15 leaves Atlanta on a march to the seaside town of Savannah. In so doing, Sherman's goal is to "make Georgia howl" by destroying resources that the Confederacy depends upon, in an effort to bring a quicker end to the war.

Some 50 miles wide North to South — between Athens and Macon, initially — the vast army lives off the land, cutting a swath of destruction as they proceed. Cattle and food crops are confiscated, while many sawmills, foundries, cotton gins and warehouses are destroyed.

The federals encounter little military resistance. The state capital of Milledgeville falls before Sherman on Nov. 23. Slaves are liberated daily. Southern morale, or what is left of it, plummets. Sherman's name quickly becomes a byword in the state. And still the march continues.

With Union victory over the Confederacy increasingly assured, what will the future of the South look like? Hints of what might be can be found up and down the Southern coast, where a number of freedmen's villages have been established in Union-controlled areas. One such place is St. Augustine, Fla., where Northern Baptist minister I.W. Brinckerhoff is the government-appointed superintendent of the work among freedmen. Brinckherhoff reports:

> The Nat. Freedmens Association have at this post, four excellent and fully
> competent teachers of the colored school. Their schools are confessedly equal
> to any in the Department and surprising progress is being made.

Lincoln remains president of the United States, Sherman's march is casting a wide net of destruction in the Southern heartland, Gen. Robert E. Lee's Army of Northern Virginia is stretched ever thinner in the trenches of Petersburg, youth gangs plague the Confederate capital, some two-thirds of Confederate soldiers have deserted the army while many others are hospitalized, tens of thousands of former slaves are being taught to read and are learning how to live as freemen, and a harsh winter with a severe shortage of food supplies in the Confederate armies and on the home front looms close.

If the Confederate States ever needed a miracle of biblical proportions, now is the time.

DECEMBER 1864

For the Confederate States of America, the month of December is one of wrenching horrors. The devastation, in the Battle of Nashville, of the one remaining large Confederate army in the Deep South is followed by the even more traumatic fall of Savannah.

From Milledgeville, Ga., Sherman's armies march steadily southeastward largely unopposed, pillaging and torching infrastructure, confiscating livestock and crops, freeing slaves and garnering the hatred of white citizens. Union forces encounter little resistance. Lopsided battles take place at Waynesboro and Fort McAllister on the approach to Savannah.

Many churches in the path of Sherman's march cancel services, as does the Bark Camp Baptist Church of Midville:

> This was the regular day for conference but owing to General William T. Sherman's Yankee Raid there was no meeting of pastors or members. We as members of Bark Camp Church do hereby place on record our solemn protest; also our thorough contempt for the vandals who desecrated our church. We are willing to leave the issue in God's hands and fervently pray that the time will come when we can worship our God under our own fig tree and have none to make us afraid.

On Dec. 21 Savannah, posing no opposition, falls to Sherman as the Union general completes his march to the sea. Sherman writes to President Lincoln: "I beg to present you as a Christmas Gift the City of Savannah, with 150 heavy guns and plenty of ammunition and also about 25,000 bales of cotton."

Celebrations of joy erupt throughout the United States as many now believe the defeat of the Confederacy is imminent.

Some white citizens stay put, resigned to occupation. The First Baptist Church remains open, one of few coastal congregations that does not close during the war. The Sunday before Sherman arrives, pastor Sylvanus Landrum preaches to a congregation of mostly Confederate soldiers stationed in the city. The Sunday following the fall of the city, Landrum preaches to a congregation largely consisting of Union soldiers.

As white Savannahans lament their ill fortune, black residents praise God and celebrate newfound freedom. The Baptist faith is predominant among blacks in Savannah, with black Baptist churches accounting for some of the most prominent African-American ministers in the South. Amid the celebrations, black Baptist leaders imagine a future of opportunity and prosperity for African Americans, a future defined by the freedom that God wills for all persons.

Many white Baptists, meanwhile, refuse to concede that slavery is unbiblical. An editorial in the North Carolina Baptist *Biblical Recorder* states the matter quite plainly, faulting whites only for not caring for the souls of their slaves.

> I have no conscientious scruples in regards to slavery; on the contrary, I believe it to be a divinely authorized institution ... much of the national distress which has fallen upon us has been permitted by God for our neglect of duty in regard to the souls of our slaves ... the sooner we appreciate and discharge our religious duties to our servants, the sooner will our calamities be past.

In Virginia, the Siege of Petersburg continues. With each passing day in the frigid trenches, hunger and despair grow among Confederate soldiers.

In Kentucky, a Baptist laywoman reflects on Confederate victories early in the war and prays for a miracle.

> I believe it was reading of [the] battles in the life of General Stonewall Jackson today that reminded me of my Father. [I] have so often in early life heard him describe the scenes of his childhood, boyhood, and youth in Culpeper. Jackson was doubtless a great and good man, but the Lord that has an undisputed right to govern all things gave him to and took him from his country and possesses all powers to raise another to fill his place. Have mercy on our guilty nation, O Lord, and with Thy strong arm drive the invaders of our soil back to their own and give us peace once more, if it be Thy will. I ask in the name of Jesus.

Amidst white Southern angst, slaves freed by Sherman's armies stream from Savannah into nearby Union-controlled Beaufort, S.C., seeking housing, education and job training offered by U.S. government officials and soldiers working in partnership with Northern missionaries. A month of unparalleled despair contrasted with great hopes thus marks the close of the year 1864.

1865

Union Gen. William T. Sherman's March to the Sea across Georgia ends at Savannah in December 1864. With both Atlanta and Savannah in Union hands, the fall of the Confederacy is mere months away. As 1865 dawns, Sherman sets his sights on Columbia and on Charleston, S.C., the birthplace of the Confederacy. Already, millions of the South's former slaves are now free. Pictured here is a group of freedmen who are tilling their own fields on Union-controlled St. Helena Island, S.C. Photo from Library of Congress.

JANUARY 1865

Celebration, chagrin and defiance alternatively greet the dawning of the new year. For free black Baptists who until recently were slaves, the first day of the year is a time of great celebration. North and South alike, black Baptist churches, having held watchnight vigils the night before in commemoration of the Emancipation Proclamation of 1863, worship, pray and praise God. Many cities, including Vicksburg and Memphis, feature community parades.

In Savannah, the newest liberated city, black clergy, many of whom are Baptist, form the Savannah Education Association that will in the weeks and months ahead create schools for blacks, taught by blacks.

Also in Savannah, on Jan. 12, Union Gen. William T. Sherman meets with 20 of the city's black ministers. The appointed spokesman for the ministers is 67-year-old former Baptist pastor Garrison Frazier, a slave until eight years prior. Sherman and Secretary of War Edwin M. Stanton pose questions to Frazier. As transcribed, a few of the questions and answers are:

Second. State what you understand by slavery, and the freedom that was to be given by the President's proclamation.

Answer. Slavery is receiving by irresistible power the work of another man, and not by his consent. The freedom, as I understand it, promised by the proclamation is taking us from under the yoke of bondage and placing us where we could reap the fruit of our own labor and take care of ourselves and assist the Government in maintaining our freedom.

Third. State in what manner you think you can take care of yourselves, and how can you best assist the Government in maintaining your freedom.

Answer. The way we can best take care of ourselves is to have land, and turn in and till it by our labor — that is, by the labor of the women, and children, and old men — and we can soon maintain ourselves and have something to spare; and to assist the Government the young men should enlist in the service of the Government, and serve in such manner as they may be wanted. (The rebels told us that they piled them up and made batteries of them, and sold them to Cuba, but we don't believe that.) We want to be placed on land until we are able to buy it and make it our own.

Fourth. State in what manner you would rather live, whether scattered among the whites or in colonies by yourselves?

Answer. I would prefer to live by ourselves, for there is a prejudice against us in the South that will take years to get over, but I do not know that I can answer for my brethren. [All but one express agreement with Frazier.]

Four days after the interview with Frazier, Sherman orders that each freed family be given 40 acres of tillable land along the South Carolina coast.

Remaining enslaved Baptists grow more confident of their impending freedom. White Baptists of the North celebrate the advance of freedom.

White Baptists of the South, however, have mixed feelings. Some now welcome the prospects of Union victory. Others, especially Georgia residents victimized by Sherman's armies, yet harbor deep-seated anger against the North. Many remain defiant, as certain as ever that slavery is God's will for the black race.

In Georgia, editor Samual Boykin expresses the sentiments of many. "The war which afflicts us has a manifest connection with slavery ... the relation between the master and the slave has the divine sanction," Boykin warns those who may be wavering. Whereas 1864 was "one long year of disaster and distress to the Confederacy," better days lie ahead if the people of God humble themselves, submit to providence, and honor God's Confederate nation and his holy name. "Have faith in your God and your cause: the one is kind and benignant — the other worthy of all effort, all sacrifice, all suffering." Fight "for all that is right, holy and just; have faith in the nobility of your cause."

A writer for the South Carolina *Confederate Baptist* insists the war is going well, evidenced by army revivals in the South and an increase of evil in the North. The future bodes well for the white people of the Confederacy, to whom will be "entrusted the custody of pure religion as well as constitutional liberty." Of the abolitionist North, "God has judged them. The prophecy of their doom is it not written in their own acts."

The editor of the Virginia Baptist *Religious Herald* also voices confidence in the Confederacy. "If a feeling of despondency with regard to the issue of the struggle for Southern independence has gone abroad among our people, we do not share it. There is no sufficient reason for this gloom that we can see."

Perhaps the eyes of many white Baptists of the South are willingly closed to the realities at hand. On Jan. 15, Fort Fisher in North Carolina near Wilmington falls to the Union. Four days later, Sherman begins moving north into South Carolina. And on Jan. 31, the U.S. House passes the 13th Amendment (the Senate already having done so) abolishing slavery, the document now ready for President Abraham Lincoln's signature and ratification by individual states.

FEBRUARY 1865

As winter chills sweep across a rapidly sinking Confederacy, three more major Southern cities fall to Union forces in rapid succession. Within the space of a week, both of South Carolina's major cities — Columbia and Charleston — fall with little resistance, as does Wilmington, N.C.

Black Baptist minister Charles H. Corey describes the scene when the victorious 54th Massachusetts Colored Regiment marches into Charleston:

> It was the first body of colored men in arms seen in this city. The boys ran, and old men laughed and cried for joy; hats were swung, aprons and handker-chiefs waved. I saw young women dancing, the older ones shouting and praising God. I stood and wept; so did many a rough soldier; so did some of the citizens of Charleston. The negroes shook hands, and clung to the soldiers and seemed almost wild with delight.

The capture of the three cities further consolidates Union control over much of the South. Other than the interior of North Carolina and much of Virginia, the Confederacy is effectively subdued. All that remains is to capture the Southern capital of Richmond.

With the end of the Confederacy in sight, last-minute peace talks between the North and South fail. To the surprise of no one, slavery is the sticking point. U.S. President Abraham Lincoln, having on Feb. 1 signed the 13th Amendment abolishing slavery, refuses Confederate demands of the continuation of Southern slavery as a condition of peace.

Lincoln's approval puts the 13th Amendment to the states for ratification. Eighteen states ratify by the end of the month, while Tennessee moves in that direction as voters enact a new constitution ending slavery.

White voices in the South, many shrill as ever in defending slavery as God's will for the black race and encouraging their white brethren to pray hard and endure in the fight, nonetheless fade into the background. Prominent news-paper editors are silenced as the South Carolina *Confederate Baptist* and North Carolina Baptist *Biblical Recorder* are both shuttered by the end of the month. Hundreds of church buildings throughout the South now stand abandoned.

Into the vacuum step black Baptist leaders in the South, many recently freed from bondage by advancing Union armies. Most prominent among these new spokesmen for Baptists are freedmen along the Georgia and South Carolina coast, particularly from Savannah to Beaufort.

This new Baptist narrative first flared brightly in the days following the Union capture of Savannah in December 1864. Rev. Garrison Frazier, retired Baptist pastor, and Rev. Ulysses L. Houston, pastor of Savannah's Third African Baptist Church, quickly emerged as leaders of the city's newly-freed black population. The city's black Baptist churches now serve, in addition to Sunday worship, as community centers for freedmen, venues for black-operated schools and headquarters of black political advocacy.

The city's white churches are also utilized by freedmen. This month Union Gen. Rufus Saxton, speaking to an audience of some 1,000 black citizens crowded into Savannah's (white) Second Baptist Church, explains that the government will provide 40 acres of land for free to each black family.

The Beaufort region, designated as a major area of black resettlement, is already experiencing an influx. Since early January, so many freedmen have arrived from Savannah that Union-operated facilities have been overwhelmed. One volunteer sadly reports of "fifteen hundred wretches without shirts or blankets, huddled like pigs in old cow-sheds, under public buildings, and on the sunny side of any wall or fence they can find, — dying by scores, of cold, and diseases caused by cold."

By some estimates, more than a thousand have already died due to exposure and the squalid conditions. Union military personnel and Northern relief workers laboring along the coast struggle to meet the great demands placed upon them as each day a hundred or more newcomers arrive.

Virginia, meanwhile, remains starkly divided. In Union-controlled Portsmouth, black Baptists openly form the Zion Baptist Church. Black Baptists in Richmond, yet enslaved, furtively meet near a trash dump to worship God, fearing beatings if discovered. Their secretive gatherings are the beginnings of the city's Fifth Baptist Church.

In what remains of the Confederacy, the month ends with such national desperation that officials are cognitively resigned to the arming of slaves. Gen. Robert E. Lee, now in charge of the entirety of the South's armies, declares: "I think the measure not only expedient, but necessary." In a gut-wrenching blow to the Confederacy's very identity, military service would earn freedom for slaves.

Finally, Northern black Baptists are seemingly inspired by the developments of recent months. Many U.S. cities yet retain racially discriminatory laws. In Chicago, black Baptists play a crucial role in this month's repeal of the city's Black Laws.

The rising crest of victory over Southern slavery, to the joy of many black Baptists throughout the North, is softening long-held racism and prejudices in the larger Union.

MARCH 1865

The sun is setting on the Confederate States of America. With most of the South now under Union control, calls from Confederate officials and religious leaders to never give up appear to ignore reality and defy logic.

Confederate Gen. Robert E. Lee, knowing the hour is near, contacts Union Gen. Ulysses S. Grant in hopes of convening a meeting to "iron out the differences" between the North and the South. The North, however, having effectively won the war, has no interest in negotiation. Instead, U.S. President Abraham Lincoln addresses the future in his second inaugural address, the last paragraph invoking God's help in finishing the fight and, afterward, in healing America's wounds:

> With malice toward none, with charity for all, with firmness in the right as God gives us to see the right, let us strive on to finish the work we are in, to bind up the nation's wounds, to care for him who shall have borne the battle and for his widow and his orphan, to do all which may achieve and cherish a just and lasting peace among ourselves and with all nations.

Part of the envisioned national healing takes the form of helping former slaves transition into lives of freedom and opportunity, to which the Freedman's Bureau, established this month, is tasked. Tens of thousands, perhaps hundreds of thousands, of black Baptists acquire help from the bureau in the months and years to come.

Before freedom can fully reign, however, remaining Confederate armed forces must be subdued. Early in the month, Union armies expand their control in North Carolina, in the process destroying many Baptist meeting houses and utilizing others as temporary hospitals. From sheer desperation the Confederate government allows the recruiting of "negro soldiers" to reinforce army ranks depleted by deaths and desertions. Despite an implicit understanding that military service will be rewarded with freedom, few slaves don the Confederate gray.

A bright streak of light flares ever so briefly across the darkening Southern horizon when Confederate forces momentarily break the Union line at Petersburg and drive toward the enemy's supply lines. The federals, however, easily turn back the advance and retake lost ground. By the end of the month, Union troops are close to breaking through Rebel defenses guarding the Confederate capital of Richmond.

Black Baptists South and North, while yet awaiting the culmination of the war, seize the opportunity to establish autonomous churches. Among the black Baptist congregations founded this month are: First African American Church of Evansville, Ind.; Zion Baptist Church of Portsmouth, Va.; Shiloh Missionary Baptist Church in Alexandria, Va.; and Pilgrim Rest Baptist Church in Klein, Texas. In addition, the "colored members" of the First Baptist Church of Nashville, Tenn., petition to become a separate and independent church, eventually establishing the First Baptist Church Capitol Hill.

In Savannah, black Union regiments, with Baptists well represented among the troops, arrive to assist in Reconstruction efforts. Charleston is the scene of a grand celebration led by freedmen. In both cities, thousands of former slaves are learning to read and write under the tutelage of missionaries from the North and other charity workers and, in some cases, local black Baptist leaders. Good and kind intentions notwithstanding, paternalism is common among white Northerners working among the freedmen.

Some white Baptists of the South embrace the coming end of slavery and prepare to move forward. The Cedar Fork Baptist Church in Tennessee this month resolves "that we declare a non fellowship against all aides and abetters of the rebelion until satisfaction be made by them to the church in the letter and spirit of the Gospel." A judge writing in the Georgia Baptist *Christian Index* concedes that African slavery may be doomed, not because it is against the will of God, but because slave marriages have not been legally recognized and honored in the South.

Other white Southern Baptists, however, remain as confident as ever. White supremacy and black slavery are the unchanging will of God. The South may not be winning on the battlefield, but the many religious conversions that have been wrought in the armies of the South represent an even greater victory.

"Triumph and joy, suffering and sorrow, hardships and peril, have all brought us near to our Maker; and the greater our peril — the more severe our calamities, the more have we felt the nearness of God," declares a newspaper editorial. Embedded within this narrative of righteous victory despite earthly defeat is a post-war path for a decimated South, a rewriting of history that, upending logic, transforms losers into victors undaunted in their divine mission of upholding white supremacy.

During these final days of the Confederacy, with the Reconstruction of some Southern states already underway, it remains to be seen whether Lincoln's hope of "malice toward none" and "charity for all" will overcome inherent racism both North and South, much less the biblically-infused militant white supremacy that drove the nation into war and even now defies defeat.

APRIL 1865

Like a towering, thundering wave crashing upon the shore, the army of U.S. Gen. Ulysses S. Grant finally breaks through the Confederate lines at Petersburg on the morning of the second day of the month, a Sunday.

It is the moment the North has long awaited, and the moment long dreaded by Confederate officials. Having rolled up Rebel defenses, the road to Richmond is open.

Within hours a telegram is delivered to Confederate President Jefferson Davis, who is attending a Sunday morning church service. The message is from the commander of the South's armies, Gen. Robert E. Lee: "I advise that all preparation be made for leaving Richmond tonight."

Jumping up, Davis rushes to his office and instructs officials to destroy government documents and then leave town. Stacks of papers are hauled outside and set ablaze.

Startled observers see the flames. As the smoke drifts skyward, rumors begin swirling around town. Something is wrong. Has the fighting at Petersburg been renewed?

At four o'clock in the afternoon the departure of the Confederate government is formally announced. Mayhem immediately ensues.

From late afternoon through the night, Richmond's white elites stream out of town. On horseback, in train cars and carriages and skiffs and boats, or pulling carts, they take what they can.

During the night, Confederate soldiers work quickly to destroy the stocks of tobacco, cotton and food stored in warehouses. When local poor whites see the massive quantities of food being brought out of secret storage, they react with disbelief, having for many months lived on the edge of starvation because of Confederate officials' insistence that there was a shortage of food.

An enraged crowd quickly forms and begins looting at will. Amid the looting, soldiers set fire to tobacco and cotton bales. The flames mingle with those from piles of government documents yet burning.

The wind picks up, spreading the flames to the business district. Loaded shells at the ironworks go off, then the arsenals aboard docked warships explode with such force that windows are shattered for a radius of two miles.

The morning of April 3 dawns on a city devastated, and devoid of many of its leading white citizens. U.S. President Abraham Lincoln is notified.

"Thank God," the president responds. "I have lived to see this! It seems to me that I have been dreaming a horrid dream for four years, and now the nightmare is gone. I want to see Richmond."

Union troops march into the city to the cheers of blacks who were slaves just hours earlier. The sight of black troops brings joyous tears to the eyes of many.

The arrival of Lincoln on April 4, however, elicits the greatest response of all. Instantly recognizing the president, former slaves greet the man who is widely viewed as their Moses.

Adm. David D. Porter, accompanying Lincoln, describes the scene: "As far as the eye could see, the streets were alive with negroes and poor whites rushing in our direction. ... They all wanted to shake hands with Mr. Lincoln or [touch] his coat tail or even to kneel down and kiss his boots!"

With Richmond fallen, Lee surrenders to Grant on April 9 at Appomattox, Va. Although some Confederate forces remain afield and Jefferson Davis is not captured until weeks later, the war is effectively over.

The rebellious states have been defeated, the Union preserved. Four long, agonizing years and more than 600,000 deaths have been required to fulfill the promises of 1776 that bound the original colonies together.

"All men are created equal," the "unanimous Declaration of the 13 united States of America" had boldly decreed back then. "Liberty" is an inherent "right." And "whenever any Form of Government becomes destructive of these ends, it is the Right of the People to alter or to abolish it," the Declaration had trumpeted.

The Southern states had denied these very words of the nation's founders, insisting that liberty belonged to whites only. For almost a century Southern white elites had enriched themselves off of slave labor, preaching white solidarity while leaving crumbs to common white folk and censuring dissenting voices.

Many Baptist elites in the South had joined the chorus, sanctifying black slavery with a literal interpretation of the Bible while condemning evil Northerners, including Baptists, who insisted that God willed freedom for all people.

The South had gone to war with the North for the stated purpose of preserving black slavery. But God's hand ultimately found expression in Northern military might, bestowing freedom to all and thus completing the American Revolution — or so many Northerners believe as celebrations erupt throughout the North.

As joyful as are Northerners, the bitterness and despair of many white Southerners is every bit as visceral. An actor and Confederate sympathizer named John Wilkes Booth, hateful of Lincoln as have been many Southerners during the war, seeks revenge.

On April 14, five days after Lee's surrender, Booth assassinates the president, shocking the world. Seemingly no one is left untouched by the murder.

Northerners are outraged and deeply saddened. In the days and weeks following the killing, from many Baptist pulpits in the North, black and white alike, flow tributes to Lincoln for his sacrificial commitment to freedom. On the other hand, many white Southerners believe Lincoln got what he deserved. Others, especially the poor, mourn.

Blacks everywhere are shocked, while many are fearful. God's agent, their deliverer, is dead. Might their newfound freedom somehow be snatched away?

Nonetheless, celebrations of freedom are held in many black Baptist churches. Former slaves praise God and Lincoln's Republican Party. At an April 23 gathering at the State Street Baptist Church in Mobile, Ala., the packed crowd of former slaves sings:

> Free workmen in the cotton-field,
> And in the sugar cane;
> Free children in the common school,
> With nevermore a chain.
> Then rally, Black Republicans —
> Aye, rally! We are free!
> We've waited long
> To sing the song —
> The song of liberty

The immediate post-war years are full of promise and hope for black citizens in the South and North. The 13th Amendment formally ends slavery in December 1865, while the 14th and 15th amendments in the years following extend legal protections to blacks and decree that suffrage cannot be predicated on the basis of race.

En masse in the South, black Baptists leave white churches and form hundreds, then thousands, of autonomous congregations. Some individuals, such as South Carolinian and war hero Robert Smalls, become political leaders in state houses and in Washington, D.C.

Others, having served in the Union military, trade their soldier uniforms for clerical garments. Collectively, black Baptists establish denominational structures to help in the tasks of missions, education and uplift of the black race. Many Northern Baptists, black and white alike, provide assistance.

White Southerners confront a land destroyed and a society, culture and economy devoid of slave labor. Southern Baptists face the daunting prospects of rebuilding their churches and denomination, eventually emerging organizationally stronger than ever.

Southern ideologues, meanwhile, set about turning defeat into victory. Unwilling to concede that the South was in the wrong in going to war with the North, they create a narrative of righteousness.

Southern Baptist leaders such as John William Jones, well-known Confederate chaplain and denominational administrator, play prominent roles in this task. Ignoring the historical records of the Confederacy that clearly portrayed the South as going to war to preserve black slavery, Jones and other Southern apologists create a "Lost Cause" mythology, recasting the war as a noble and moral fight for states rights and Southern traditions.

While the godless North won the war due to military dominance, the superior Southern way of life had not been conquered. Quietly set aside in public discourse is the fact that "states rights" and the "traditional" Southern "way of life" were shorthand for black slavery. The new narrative thus preserves white supremacy while downplaying slavery.

Nonetheless, many remain convinced that God yet wills that the black race be subservient to the white. Some openly voice such sentiments. In the 1890s Southern Baptists support efforts to take freedoms away from blacks, including the implementation of apartheid laws and the suppression of black votes.

The end of the war, it turns out, is anything but. Not only are blacks in the post-war South gradually stripped of many of the freedoms to which they are legally entitled as American citizens, but racism remains all too real in the post-war North.

The Civil War was thus a second revolution, but an incomplete one. Legislatively, full freedom and equality for black citizens will not come until the passing of another 100 years.

EPILOGUE

On the 150th anniversary of the American Civil War the nation's first black president occupies the White House in his second term of office. Barack Obama's surprising rise in American politics and his historic win in the 2008 elections revealed just how far black Americans have come since the abolishment of black slavery at the end of the Civil War. Obama's presidency, however, has done little to alleviate the great divide that yet exists between white and black America.

In the United States today most white Americans own homes, while most black Americans are renters, many living in the nation's most blighted urban neighborhoods. The average black family owns about 5 percent of the wealth of the average white family. Alongside this vast economic disparity, black Americans are proportionally far more likely to be arrested than are whites. In the states of the Old Confederacy, white politicians have a solid lock on state political structures and dominate the region's representation in Washington, D.C. And, church sanctuaries North and South are the most segregated places in the nation.

In the America of 2015 and despite the amazing story of Barack Obama, white Americans as a class of citizens are advantaged in every way over black Americans, reflective of a systemic, racial bias hearkening back to antebellum days. The Civil War forced white Southerners to remove the physical shackles of black enslavement, but ultimately did not tear down the underlying ideological construct of white supremacy both South and North. Today, although America's legal system is formally color blind, social, educational and economic structures remain firmly grounded in white privilege and advantage. As of yet, there is no tangible movement toward parity.

During the Civil War, America's churches — both North and South — were an integral part of the battle to define freedom, liberty and equality. The bloody battlefields on American soil are long past, yet racism, discrimination and inequality remain a very real part of the nation's landscape. If Christianity is to play a positive role in the America of the next 150 years, a good place to start would be in helping a still-divided nation overcome the dark side of the Civil War's legacy.

SELECTED BIBLIOGRAPHY

Primary Sources, Antebellum and Civil War Era

American Baptist Records

Baptist Associational Minutes/Records*

Baptist Books*

Baptist Diaries*

Baptist Journals*

Baptist Newspapers:
>*Baptist Banner* (Ga.)
>*Biblical Recorder* (N.C.)
>*Christian Herald* (Mich.)
>*Christian Index* (Ga.)
>*Christian Reflector* (MA)
>*Confederate Baptist* (S.C.)
>*New York Examiner* (N.Y.)
>*Religious Herald* (Va.)
>*Tennessee Baptist* (Tenn.)
>*Western Recorder* (Ky.)

Baptist Sermons*

Baptist Tracts*

City Newspapers:
>*Macon Telegraph*
>*New York Times*
>*Richmond Daily Dispatch*

Local Baptist Church Minutes/Records*

Soldiers and Sailors Database, National Park Service
(http://www.nps.gov/civilwar/soldiers-and-sailors-database.htm)

Southern Baptist Convention Records

State Baptist Convention Records*

* *See civilwarbaptists.com for more information.*

SUGGESTED READING

Recent Secondary Sources

"Africans in America." Public Broadcasting Corporation. http://www.pbs.org/wgbh/aia/part1/index.html.

"Baptists and the Civil War." *Baptist History & Heritage*, 32, no. 3, no. 4 (July/October 1997).

Daly, John Patrick. *When Slavery Was Called Freedom: Evangelicalism, Proslavery and the Causes of the Civil War*. University Press of Kentucky, 2004.

"Faith, Freedom, Forgiveness: Religion and the Civil War, Emancipation and Reconciliation in Our Time." *Baptist History & Heritage*, 49, no 2 (Summer 2013).

Faust, Drew Gilpin. *The Creation of Confederate Nationalism: Ideology and Identity in the Civil War*. Louisiana State University Press, 1990.

Franklin, John Hope, and Evelyn Higginbotham. *From Slavery to Freedom: A History of African Americans*, ninth edition. McGraw-Hill, 2010

Fuller, A. James. *Chaplain to the Confederacy: Basil Manly and Baptist Life in the Old South*. Louisiana State University Press, 2000.

Genovse, Eugene D. *A Consuming Fire: The Fall of the Confederacy in the Mind of the White Christian South*. Mercer University Press, 2009.

Goen, C.C. *Broken Churches, Broken Nation*. Mercer University Press, 1997.

Gourley, Bruce T. *Diverging Loyalties: Baptists in Middle Georgia During the Civil War*. Mercer University Press, 2011.

Kelly, Joseph. *America's Longest Siege: Charleston, Slavery, and the Slow March Toward the Civil War*. Overlook Press, 2013.

Miller, Randall M., Harry S. Stout, Charles Reagan Wilson, eds. *Religion and the American Civil War.* Oxford University Press, 1997.

Noll, Mark. *The Civil War as Theological Crisis.* University of North Carolina Press, 2006.

Rable, George C. *God's Almost Chosen Peoples: A Religious History of the American Civil War.* University of North Carolina Press, 2010.

Richard, Roger Charles. *Actions and Attitudes of Southern Baptists Toward Blacks, 1845-1895.* Dissertation, Florida State University, 2008.

Scott, Sean A. *A Visitation of God: Northern Civilians Interpret the Civil War.* Oxford University Press, 2010.

Stout, Harry S. *Upon the Altar of the Nation: A Moral History of the Civil War.* Penguin Books, 2007.

Wesley, Timothy L. *The Politics of Faith During the Civil War.* Louisiana State University Press, 2013.

Wilson, Charles Reagan. *Baptized in Blood: The Religion of the Lost Cause, 1865-1920.* University of Georgia Press, 2009.

Woodworth, Steven E. *While God Is Marching On: The Religious World of Civil War Soldiers.* University of Kansas Press, 2001.

CPSIA information can be obtained
t www.ICGtesting.com
inted in the USA
W03n1825081016
FS